No. 2001
$7.95

Automobile Restoration Guide 2nd Edition

BY STANLEY NOWAK

FOR ALL ANTIQUE, CLASSIC, SPECIAL INTEREST,
AND MILESTONE CARS.

MODERN SPORTS CAR SERIES

TAB BOOKS

Blue Ridge Summit, Pa. 17214

SECOND EDITION

FIRST PRINTING—DECEMBER 1977

Copyright 1977 by TAB BOOKS

Printed In the United States
of America

Library of Congress Cataloging in Publication Data

Nowak, Stanley, 1903-
　Automobile restoration guide, for all antique, classic, special
interest.

　(Modern sports car series)
　　1. Automobiles—Restoration. I. Title.
TL152.2.N68 1977 629.28'8'22 77-25533
ISBN 0-8306-9994-5
ISBN 0-8306-2001-X pbk.

Cover photo courtesy by Ford Motor Company.

Contents

Acknowledgements

Special thanks for helping produce this book are due to:

Road & Track for publishing the article which inspired this volume.

Don Lefferts, Manager, Vintage Auto Restorations Inc., Ridgefield, Connecticut, who supplied many of the photographs and contributed his knowledge and experience.

Robert Turnquist, Manager, Hibernia Auto Restorations Inc., Hibernia, New Jersey, who supplied photographs.

Ernest and Bob Swanson, Ridgefield, Connecticut, for their help and cooperation on Model A matters.

Chuck Nesbitt, Restoration Manager of Grand Prix SSR Co., E. Setauket, Long Island, New York, who helped in revising this book.

Introduction

If you're past the point of deciding to buy an old car and past the point of searching for and acquiring the old car of your dreams, you're ready to explore the multitudinous mysteries of restoration. For you, it's too late to reconsider. You're committed. And this book will help you decide if you should do the work yourself, have it done professionally, or strike a middle course, some "do it yourself" and some professional work.

If you haven't yet bought that old car, you will find this book even more valuable, as it will help you decide if restoring an old car is something you should get involved in. Can you afford it? Do you have the spare time to devote to it? Do you have a place to work? Will your family be sympathetic and cooperative? How much will it cost? How much time will it require? How much research is required? How perfect does a restoration have to be? What tools will you need and how much will they cost? Where do you go to get parts required or replaced? And most important, *what* car should you restore?

In philosophical terms, this book will not dictate any "best way" of restoring an old car. It will simply give you the options and let you decide the "best way" in terms of your own personal needs, desires and limitations.

Good luck!

STONY BROOK, N.Y.
August, 1977

Stanley Nowak

Chapter 1

What to Buy: Emotion vs. Investment

Don't be afraid to buy your first old car for emotional, sentimental reasons. The most famous automobile collector in the world, Bill Harrah, bought his first car, a Maxwell, because of the happy memories he associated with it. Today, he owns the largest collection of automobiles in the world, over 1,200 of them, located in Reno, Nevada and it is well worth a detour to see.

If you do have a sentimental favorite, chances are it's a Ford. Perhaps a Model A like the one I bought in high school for $50 and sold a year later for $75! Or could it be that '36 Ford V8 Roadster you longingly admired but could never afford. Don't worry, your instincts were right. Stick to an old Ford and you'll never be hurt. Well, at least your chances of being hurt are greatly diminished.

The "old Ford" section of the hobby is enormous. Of the

estimated 250,000 car owners in the hobby, probably one third of them are involved with Fords of one kind or another. This massive interest has created a commercially important demand for Ford parts, Ford services, Ford literature, and Ford restoration specialists. Dozens of profit-minded enthusiasts have sought and discovered "New Old Stock" (NOS, as it is referred to in the classified ads). These are original, new parts made by Ford. In addition, most parts that are in demand are being reproduced. Many are so well made that they are difficult to separate from the NOS.

Even more important to you is the large and growing market involved in the buying and selling of old Fords. Literally hundreds are offered for sale every month. This amount of constant competitive activity establishes firm prices, lessens the risk of "getting stuck" and, if you should change your mind, ensures a sale at a fair price within a reasonably short time. The final argument in favor of Fords is price. An unrestored one in poor condition can be bought for as little as a few hundred dollars and finest restored Fords go for well under $15,000, about as inexpensive as you will find in the old car hobby.

If the Fords are safe investments then the riskiest cars to buy must be all those that are little known and of no technical importance. The 1905 Pungs Finch (owned by Austin Clark's Long Island Automotive Museum, Southhampton, New York) is certainly a little known car but it is very valuable because of its superb workmanship, heroic size (610 cubic inches), and advanced engineering features (overhead valves and overhead camshaft).

The real losers are the dozens of uninteresting, inexpensive, assembled cars that were ground out in the U.S. between 1915 and 1930. At the risk of offending some owners I must list a few of the cars which are noteworthy for their total lack of redeeming features: Corinthian, Drummond, Fremont, Hackett, Huffman, Marshall, and Olympian are some of the makes in this category. Their lack of desirability

---

A safe investment! A lovely 1931 Model A Ford Roadster restored for "show or go" by the owner. Owner: Ernest Swanson, Ridgefield, Conn.

is not enhanced by their rarity. This is the type of car which is least interesting to the collector. Parts are almost impossible to obtain and resale may take years.

Between the Fords and the Fremonts is a vast middle ground of well made, well engineered automobiles, some with ingenious technical features, which are well worth restoring provided you have the patience and determination to see them through to completion: don't pass up a car because you never heard of it. First, look it up in The Complete Encyclopedia of Motor Cars, edited by G.N. Georgano, available in most libraries. This will give you a thumbnail sketch of the car's history and unusual features, a basis on which to judge its potential. More detailed information will have to be obtained from owners of the particular make, editors of club magazines, club specialists, and libraries specializing in automobiles such as the Detroit Public Library, automotive history collection, 5201 Woodward Ave., Detroit, Mich. 48202.

If you are able to invest in one of the "great classics," you may find it rewarding to talk to a professional in the field of buying and selling the best old cars, such as Ed Jurist, who owns the Vintage Car Store in Nyack, N.Y. and who has steered his steady customers into the great cars for over a dozen years. Mr. Jurist keeps a file on every car he has sold and these records document the monumental extent of his foresight. He strongly recommends the purchase of cars which were acknowledged "the best" when they were new; cars fitted with the bodywork of the most outstanding coachbuilders of their day, cars that were acknowledged as outstanding for their workmanship and engineering. A definitive list of these "great cars" is not possible, for as the list grows the selection becomes more subjective and the choice more financially speculative. Rolls Royce, Bentley, Duesenberg, Packard, Mercedes, Cadillac, Bugatti, Stutz, Mercer, Simplex are undisputed great cars but even a Rolls Royce can be a poor investment if it is the low powered 20HP model bearing 4-door sedan coachwork that is aesthetically displeasing. The sex appeal of the coachwork is an important factor in determining present value and future appreciation. The most desirable are the 4-door touring cars and the dual-cowl phaetons (with a windshield for the rear passengers as well as the front) are the ultimate in this category. From this pinnacle the order of value descends: roadster, convertible, coupe, town car, sedan, limousine, hearse.

Unquestionably, the "great cars" are the best investments. Over the past ten years Duesenbergs have appreciated over 1,000%! So have Bugattis. These are among the "classic cars," as defined by the Classic Car Club of America. This well organized national club specializes in cars made between 1925 and World War II and the list of cars which they have decided are "classic" is at the back of Appendix II.

If you are fortunate enough to have a lot of money to invest in old cars you will do well to consider buying only the most expensive ones! Over the past twenty years, every car which sold at a record price at the time has appreciated 5 to 10 times as much as the average old cars sold at the same time! A Duesenberg Coupe de Ville which sold for $5,000 in 1960 was sold recently for $95,000. A Type 59 Grand Prix Bugatti bought for $7,500 in 1962 is now worth $200,000 . A Bugatti Type 57SC Atlantic sold at auction only five years ago for $69,000 is worth over $125,000 today. If you can afford it you can own and enjoy the finest classic knowing it will appreciate in value faster than any other car, and for that matter, faster than most other forms of investment. Indeed, great automobiles are as important as great paintings, gold coins, and land as an investment medium.

If you don't have vast quantities of excess cash to invest in a verified "classic" and prefer something at a lower price, albeit more speculative, you might find the post-war period more interesting. The Milestone Car Society specializes in this period with a cutoff after 1964 and a list of their certified "milestone" cars is included at the back of Appendix II. In a sense, The Milestone Society is trying to guess which of the more recently produced cars will become true classics in the future. To help them with the guessing game they have entrusted the selection of "milestone" cars to a board of distinguished experts whose choices are finally approved or disapproved by a vote of the membership. If you agree with them and want to back it up with cash you can start buying 1949 and 1963 Buick Rivieras, any Rolls Royce, 1961 through 1964 Lincoln Continentals, 1953 through 1956 Packard Caribbeans, and so on. The full list is a great conversation piece as it never fails to arouse disagreement. From an investment point of view it presents most interesting possibilities. The stakes are not too high and if you guess right, the rewards can be great. Meanwhile, you have a car which can be used for every day transportation, if you can preserve it at the same time.

If post-war cars appeal to you, The Milestone Car Society is not the only game in town. For example, the Vintage Sports Car Club of America encourages the preservation of post-war sport/racing cars by issuing a list of those "eligible" to compete in their hill climbs, races, and concours. Most rare and unusual sports cars and racing cars made before January 1, 1960 are on the "eligible" list (available on request from the secretary of the club). The activities of this club together with the clubs in England who sponsor post-war "historic" racing has seen a steady appreciation in values. Ferrari racing models which were once available for $3,500 or less are today fetching $10,000 and more. Even small displacement racing cars such as the Lotus XI and Lola 1100 are selling for $5500 to $15,000 whereas three or four years ago they could be had for under $1,000.

One make clubs devoted to post-war cars are in abundance. Ferraris were not made before World War II and there are three good clubs devoted to their cause. For the well-heeled post-war enthusiast, the Ferrari is probably the best choice. In particular, the rarer sports-racing models seem destined for maximum appreciation. If Ferraris appeal to you, join all their clubs, plunge in and learn all you can before you buy. Yes, there are Ferraris you can buy in good working condition for $6500 or less but they are not necessarily the models that will appreciate the most.

Ideally, you should be able to combine an emotional choice, the car you have secretly longed for, with a car you believe will be worth more to others in the future. For most of us, the final choice will be a compromise. It must be a car whose purchase you can defend with enthusiasm. If "maximum potential appreciation" is not important to you, don't worry about it. The only lost cause in the world of automobiles is when the owner loses his enthusiasm. Bill Harrah's first Maxwell is still part of his world famous collection and, of course, it is worth more today than when he bought it.

Chapter 2

Car Restoration: Time, Money and Space

Most professional car restoration shops charge $15 or more per hour for their labor plus the cost of materials or services purchased outside, to which they usually add 20% for handling. If unusually hard-to-find parts are missing you will have to pay the professional restorer for the time he devotes to finding the parts, at $15 per hour, plus the cost of the parts themselves. Or you will have to pay the cost of having them made. If the part is machined the machinest will charge at least $18 per hour plus the cost of the raw material. If you can do some or all of this work yourself you will save a lot of money. You can replace money spent with a professional restoration service with your own time.

If your own time and money are limited you save a great deal of both by buying an old car which is 100% complete and original. This means doing some homework before you go out to buy. Yes, this may even mean passing up a "bargain" until you know what you are buying. In the case of a very rare and unusual car this homework is vital. Not long ago, a friend who works for a professional restoration shop drove from New York to Boston to buy what was represented to be a 1913 Peugeot "Bebe" Roadster. What he found was a very early Austin 7 worth far less! Fortunately, he had worked on a genuine Peugeot "Bebe" and knew the car intimately. This kind of deception is rare but it does happen. If you have a limited bankroll it can be disastrous.

The quickest way to become an "expert" on a particular make of car is to buy all the books available on the subject and join the clubs that cater to your car. Books can be ordered from the specialist book dealers listed in Appendix III and the clubs are listed in Appendix II. To get the most help join two clubs: 1) a club devoted exclusively to your make of car and, 2) a more general club that accepts all cars of a particular era. Several examples: if you plan to buy a 1938 Packard 180, join the Packard Owners Club and the Classic Car Club of America (the 180 model Packard is a "classic" as defined by the CCCA); if you desire a 1925 Ford Model T, join the Model T Ford Club International and the Antique Automobile Club of America or the Horseless Carriage Club, depending on which has the most active chapter in your area; if the 1951-54 Hudson Hornet is your choice, join the Hudson-Essex-Terraplane Club and the Milestone Car Society, which specializes in post-war cars and defines the 1951-54 Hudson Hornet as a "milestone car;" if you're planning to restore a 1946-49 M.G.T.C. you will want to join the M.G. "T" Register, the Vintage Sports Car Club of America, and the Milestone Car Society. A full list of the cars accepted by the Classic Car Club of America and The Milestone Car Society is included in the back of Appendix II.

Study the books you have acquired and attend the meetings of the clubs you have joined. When, at a meeting, you see a car of the type you want to buy, introduce yourself to the owner as a new member and ask him to show you his car. Most owners are delighted to show off their cars and their expertise. If you feel you are getting along well with the owner, ask him for his name, address, and phone number. When you are ready to buy your old car you may find that your new friend is willing to go with you to inspect the car. You will certainly find his experience invaluable in selecting a car and during the time the car is being restored.

Ideally, you want a car that is 100% complete and running. But does it really have to be 100% original? Who cares if the carburetor is a modern replacement? It probably works better anyway.

Here we must define the purpose of collecting old cars. In simplest terms, it is to preserve them. An old car is not preserved by substituting a modern carburetor for the original. Improving an old car is not necessarily preserving it. The car clubs are devoted to preserving old cars and there is no place for the 1936 Cord with a Cadillac engine in it or a 1928 Model A Ford with hydraulic brakes. Old cars that have been extensively modified should be avoided. For the most part, such cars provide only "show off" transportation and contribute nothing to the hobby or to the preservation of automobile history. We are not referring to the classic hot rod or street rod. These are legitimate facets of the automotive hobby but have no relationship to the subject of this book, the restoration and preservation of old cars.

From the standpoint of saving time and money, the perfect car to buy would be one which had been properly stored in a heated garage while it was still in "as new" original condition. Such a car would require no restoration, only further preservation! Find a car as close to this "ideal" as possible. Think ahead and you will buy with care and patience, looking for the very best in originality and condition.

Chapter 3

How To Buy An Old Car: Restored and Unrestored

Anyone with experience in the hobby (or business) of buying old cars will tell you the need is for plenty of hard cash, persistence, and luck. Let's consider the situation honestly. There's nothing like a roll of bills counted out on a table to separate a man from his long loved but neglected automotive treasure. And this is exactly the kind of factor needed when you're trying to buy an old car that is *not* for sale. This is the toughest "buy" in the world. Sometimes, money alone will do it, if you have enough, but more than likely it will take something more. If you can talk to the owner you will probably be wise to pull out all the emotional stops. If you've heard of the car from a friend or neighbor you'll want a personal introduction. Find out what the owner likes, what his interests are and make use of the information. Anything you can do to assure the owner that the car will be a tribute to him is bound to help. Let him know that the car will be restored to "as new" running condition and that it will be displayed at public events with a sign giving the full history of the car and his part in its preservation.

Arrive at the owner's home in a restored old car and you will do wonders to convince him of the credibility of your story. How can anyone not be swayed by the sight of a beautiful old car which looks and runs as perfectly as the day it left the factory?

Fortunately, there are plenty of old car owners who are delighted to sell their cars and these people are much easier to cope with. These cars are advertised in small local newspapers, local "buy-lines" and "mart" papers, local auto club bulletins, and in the national publications such as *Hemming's Motor News, Cars and Parts, Old Cars, Road and Track, The New York Times, Motor Sport* (published in England), and the national auto club bulletins and magazines.

Hemming's Motor News is probably the best all round source for old cars and parts of all types. This magazine has a circulation of over 144,000 and consists of over 220 pages of classified ads with almost no editorial matter. Over half the cars offered are Fords or post-war milestone or special-interest cars (made after World War II that are not recognized by any of the major old car clubs). The rest covers the entire spectrum of automobiles made in the world. Even if you don't find the car you want, you will find Hemming's a fascinating treasure trove of automobilia of every description. For sheer quantity of old cars for sale there is nothing like it.

Cars and Parts also offer pages of classified ads similar in coverage to Hemming's but with many pages of valuable editorial material, car make histories, reprints of car catalogs, etc., and it printed on a good grade of glossy paper.

Old Cars is *the* newspaper of the old car hobby. In it you will find the best coverage of what the clubs are doing, what is happening at the old car auctions, with lists of exactly what cars are sold and for how much. It also reviews new books and includes a large section of classified ads of cars, parts, and services. If you want to subscribe to only one general publication, it is probably the best one.

Road and Track is a well-known national car enthusiast's magazine. Of all the national magazines available on news stands everywhere it has by far the largest classified section of cars for sale. Those offered are almost entirely sports cars or luxury cars made in Europe and for this type of car it is probably the best source.

The New York Times, Sunday Edition, Sports Section contains the automobile classified ads. Between the late model American cars and late model foreign cars is a section headed "Antique & Classic Cars," which is the largest section of its kind in any newspaper in America. Cars of every conceivable type are offered and most serious collectors in the Northeast spend every Sunday morning reading it before anything else. It is also available a day or two later in every large city in the country.

Motor Sport magazine, published in England, is a must for every foreign car lover. In addition to excellent editorial coverage of old car activities in Great Britain it also offers a very large classified section of Rolls Royces, Bentleys, and every other make of European car. Single copies are available from R. Gordon & Co. (see under "Books and Manuals" in Appendix III).

Club magazines and bulletins are highly recommended as many club members will offer their cars first in a club publication. Particularly valuable are the magazines and bulletins offered by the Antique Automobile Club of America, the Classic Car Club of America, the Horseless Carriage Club, and the Veteran Motor Car Club of America.

When you find a car advertised that appeals to you, telephone and ask for details of the condition of the car. Be certain to get the correct year of the car, model, type and number, and its chassis and engine numbers. This information can be invaluable when discussing the car with owners of similar automobiles or other experts on that make. If the car is at a distant location ask for photographs. If no telephone number is given in the advertisement you will have to write the owner but it is always better to telephone since you may want to ask the owner to hold the car for you based on the information you receive from him. A deposit of $50 to $100 will usually hold a car until you can obtain the photographs and full information on which you can base your decision to proceed with it or not.

Photographs can be very misleading. They always make a poor car look good and a perfect car look average. Either way, you don't get a true picture of the car's condition from them. Moral: Don't buy any car without inspecting it personally and thoroughly.

When you go to buy the car be prepared to pay for it in full with a certified check, cash, or traveler's checks. Do not pay for a car unless you can take delivery immediately. Come prepared with a car trailer, tow bar, or, if driveable, license plates. If the owner says the car is in running condition make it clear to him that you will want to hear the engine and have a demonstration ride before buying it. Bring a mechanic familiar with the car or the owner of a similar one and let the owner know that you will make a total and careful inspection.

Before you begin a mechanical check, find out exactly what, if anything, is not original on the car. This means a thorough survey of the car from top to bottom inside and out. Don't hesitate to bring your research material with you. Take your time, paying close and particular attention to lights, engine and transmission, rear axle, instruments, wheels (checking for correct original size), and bumpers.

Most important (and this is often overlooked) is the maker's plate on the firewall. This plate is usually stamped with the engine and chassis numbers (often two different numbers). Bring a flashlight and be sure the number stamped on the engine is the same as the "Engine Number" on the plate. If it is not the same it is very possible the engine may be unacceptable for the use in club events. This means you will have to identify the engine before you can decide if the car can be considered original. In cases like this you should get a ruling from the club to find out what is acceptable and what is not.

Once you are satisfied that the car is original you can proceed to a study of its condition. If the car is represented as being in good mechanical condition you should check the following:

1) If the radiator is cold and the car starts quickly you can be sure the engine is in reasonably good condition.

2) A drive of 20 minutes or more is advisable in order to be certain the cooling system is in good order and that the oil pressure is satisfactory (oil pressure information should be obtained from the owner of a similar car). This will give you the opportunity to observe the functioning of the gear shift (always ask to have the car driven in reverse for a few feet), the clutch, brakes, horn, instruments, and emergency brake (on a hill, please). Oil pressure should be steady (erratic or low oil pressure could indicate bearings about to expire).

3) Noise in the engine, gearbox or rear axle should be evaluated by your "expert" companion. Some cars are noted for habitually noisy rear axles or valves.

4) Compression testing of each cylinder takes only a few minutes and will reveal many serious faults in the engine. If all cylinder readings are within 10% of each other it is likely the engine is in good condition. If one or more cylinders show no pressure or very low pressure compared to the others, you are in for trouble. At the very least, the valves will have to be inspected and probably the rings, which means a major overhaul.

Unless the engine has been recently overhauled or has been lovingly preserved, you must count on having it rebuilt and this should be calculated as part of the cost of restoration.

5) The "front end" is also important. Check the following:

a) "Play" in the steering. If you can move the steering wheel more than 1" at the rim before the front wheels move you will find that it is caused by a worn steering box, worn tie rod ends, or all of them.

b) Jack up the front of the car and check the amount of wear in the king-pins.

6) Check if all the instruments and lights are in good working order. Don't forget to check the heater if there is one.

The condition of the body is just as important as the mechanics of the car. For a steel bodied car, the enemy is rust.

Don't worry about the rust you can see; search for the rust that has not yet broken through to the surface and for the rust that has been patched with fiberglas or putty. Bring a magnet with you and try it in places you suspect will be rusted. This usually is where one panel joins another providing a low spot to catch water. Running boards and the panels below the doors are particularly susceptible to rust. Cars that have been patched with fiberglas or putty, revealed by a magnet, should be avoided.

Don't be fooled by cars made partly or wholly of aluminum since the magnet will not react to aluminum. Many of the more expensive foreign cars have moving panels (doors, hood, trunk) made of aluminum with the rest of steel. All aluminum bodies are usually found on one-of-a-kind prototype cars and those intended for racing, and are generally considered more valuable.

Now comes the trickiest part of the whole transaction. What should you pay for it? And a slightly different question — what is it worth? In absolute terms the "market" value of any given car is the price paid recently for an identical car. If you follow the old car auctions you will have the best idea of what current market values represent. The prices advertised in magazines and newspapers are "asking" prices and these must usually be discounted 10%-20% to find their real market value. You might try the Kruse Green Book or the Old Car Value Guide (listed under Books and Manuals in Appendix III). These list old cars sold at auction, privately, and by dealers specializing in old cars and they do their best to accurately describe the condition of the cars. But be warned, frequently the car model information is inaccurate: wrong year, wrong model, or wrong body style.

Have you thought of buying a fully restored car? If you have little time and aptitude for restoration work, a strong desire for an old car you can be proud of and a high four-figure bank balance, you should give serious consideration to a car that has been fully restored.

Consider the economics of buying a restored car. An unrestored car will take from one to two years to complete and the cost of restoration will increase 10% to 15% each year with the final cost really impossible to calculate. A fully restored car can often be bought for last year's restoration costs. One man's folly can be another man's bargain and you will know exactly what it will cost. Appreciation on a restored car will run at the rate of 10% to 20% a year. Add to this the advantages of instant enjoyment and you have a very appealing possibility.

Whatever you decide, get as much help and advice as you can, knowing full well that the final decision will be yours to make. This is when "What is it worth?" comes to grips with "What should I pay for it?" Do your homework well. Get as much expert help as you can from the most knowledgeable enthusiasts you know. The more you know about the subject the less likely you will have reason to regret your decision.

Chapter 4:
Professional Restoration: Why and How?

If you have just purchased your favorite old car in unrestored condition and have neither the time, skill nor inclination to "do it yourself" you have nothing to fear. Join the hundreds of collectors who each year entrust their out-of-date machinery to a professional restoration service.

The proper restoration of any automobile is an expensive proposition. Careful consideration should be made of the risks and advantages. Advice should be sought from experienced and objective sources. The depth of your investment should relate to the potential value of the car. Is your car really worth restoring? Are you prepared to accept a truthful, objective answer? What will professional restoration cost? What will your car be worth after it is restored?

If you ask well-known collectors with long experience in the economics of restoration you will probably find they are loath to share their experience with you. Their reluctance is understandable. They don't want to divulge their mistakes — such as too much money spent restoring the wrong car or trouble with the Internal Revenue Service who wonders if it really is a hobby. And don't forget the wife they've been deceiving for all these years who now believes her husband is going to leave her a gold mine in old cars, when most of his collection consists in worthless mid-twenties Moon, Whippet and Maxwell cars he remembered from his youth. On the other hand, he may be reluctant to admit that all his Duesenbergs were bought for $1200, restored for $5000 in the days when a dollar was worth at least 95¢ and are worth $150,000 today. His cars have appreciated so much he is embarrassed to talk about it. No doubt about it, inflation, affluence, increased demand and dwindling supply have convinced many enthusiasts that car collecting is a worthwhile investment. It is an argument that is used to justify the purchase of an old car to your wife, family and close friends. Unfortunately, it is only half true and for every great car that in time is worth two, three or four times its acquisition and restoration cost, there are 5 so-so cars that appreciate very slowly and are never worth even the cost of restoration.

After locating and surveying over 60 professional restoration services in the U.S. and Canada, I found that most of them will restore only those cars which will be worth at least the cost of restoration when the work is completed. Aside from keeping the collector on the path of restoring desirable cars, this policy protects the shop from owning a worthless car in the event of nonpayment. It also puts their restorations to the forefront in any public display of old cars; the great ones always have the largest crowds around them.

How do you find out which cars are likely to appreciate most rapidly? Become active in one or more of the national clubs suited to your interests. Study the ads in the club magazines and in those specializing in offering old cars. Talk to experienced collectors at club meetings. Follow the prices paid in auctions and the prices asked in advertisements.

If you really love old cars, you should think carefully about the responsibilities of ownership before you tow that old wreck home. Unless you're a junk collector you should have a heated garage (or one that can be heated) ready to house your new purchase. Be prepared to pay for the restoration out of surplus income. Some restoration shops, usually the larger ones, will agree to restore your car on a timetable geared to an amount you can pay each month.

What does it cost to have a professional restoration shop restore an old car? Plenty. The least expensive to restore are Fords. Some shops will fully restore a Model A Deluxe Roadster for as little as $10,000. The final price is based on the particular shop's hourly rate, plus materials. Wilkinson & Sharp (Feasterville, Pa.) estimates they can do a perfect brass radiator Model T for $20,000 to $25,000 (at a rate of $16 per hour plus materials) assuming no parts are missing and the wood and metal are still serviceable. In all cases, a professional restoration shop will remove the body and start with the bare frame. About half the total cost will be for rebuilding the engine, gearbox, rearend, and frame. Do this mechanical work yourself and you can cut the cost about in half. The larger cars, like a Simplex or a Duesenberg will cost much more; $20,000 to $30,000 is not uncommon. A figure of $60,000 is possible with a large complex car such as a supercharged Duesenberg in "basket case" condition; i.e., boxes of parts that may become a car.

Restoration outside the U.S. or Canada is a possibility. The well-known lower labor rates are attractive and a number of American aficionados have shipped their cars abroad. In the case of Rolls Royce and Bentley cars this can be advantageous as Rolls Royce will restore cars at the premises of their coachbuilding subsidiary, Park Ward, H.J. Mulliner, Ltd. and the level of their workmanship is extraordinary. The total cost will be not much less than the same work here but the quality, particularly in woodwork, will be superior.

The disadvantages of restoration abroad are numerous. Aside from Great Britain there is a language problem. The great distance involved will discourage mutual understanding on important details. Authenticity will be a problem as

A less safe investment! A professionally restored 1938 Delahaye 135MS Roadster with exotic custome coachwork by Figoni and Falaschi of Paris. It's art deco style does not appeal to everyone. Credit: Vintage Auto Restorations Inc., Ridgefield, Conn.

the Europeans don't really understand our requirements for show purposes. Any savings are usually offset by the cost of shipment both ways and insurance for the period involved.

A "cheap" restoration here or abroad is not possible. There are no magic short cuts! Potential customers looking for an inexpensive job are shown the door by any reputable restoration shop.

Are there legitimate ways of saving money on a professional restoration? Yes. Buy an unrestored car that is original, complete and with all woodwork and metal in usable condition. If you don't know dry rot from a dry Martini, take an expert with you. Without X-ray vision you won't avoid all the booby traps but you will beat most of them. If parts are missing, find them yourself and don't deliver the car for restoration until all the parts are in hand. Time you spend on chasing parts will simply lower the total cost by the number of hours involved.

Don't think you can achieve a direct saving by choosing the restoration shop with the lowest hourly rate. The hourly rate does not necessarily have anything to do with the final cost for a given car. A shop working slowly or inefficiently, charging a low rate will cost you more than a well-run shop charging more per hour. In all cases you must judge by closely examining a completed example of the work of a particular shop.

All of which brings us to the subject of how to choose the professional restoration shop for your particular car. Don't take the advice of the first enthusiastic friend whose 1910 Simplex was just beautifully restored by restoration shop "A." Your 1929 Packard will probably be done with less expense and greater authenticity by shop "B" who knows Packards intimately from long experience. Choose a shop experienced in your make of car.

Go to the club meets and talk to the owners of cars like your own. Be a good listener. Take notes. Carefully examine fully restored cars from the shops that have been recommended. Decide tentatively on one or two shops and call them for an appointment.

At this point you are about to commit your prize possession for restoration and it is wise to approach these shops with the right mental attitude. Basically, very few of them need your business. Many are booked up two to three years ahead. If you call them on the phone, you will probably detect a tone of seeming reluctance to take on your project. Don't be put off. These shops have been conditioned by frequent phone calls from "bargain hunters." It will help if you mention the name of one of their steady customers. It will help even more if you will go to see them with photos of your car and a demonstrable understanding of the problems they will be facing in restoring your car.

Money must be discussed. It is most important that you have an understanding of how and when payments are to be made. While you're at the shop, look around and ask ques-

A well organized fully equipped machine shop is a necessity for a professional restoration shop specializing in mechanical restoration work. Credit: Vintage Auto Restorations, Inc., Ridgefield, Conn.

tions. It is usually wise to choose a shop with a methodical, well-organized approach to the problems inherent in reducing a complete automobile to 10,000 individual parts and putting them back together again. It is particularly important in a large shop restoring more than three or four cars at a time. At Vintage Auto Restorations, Inc., Ridgefield, Conn. (specializing in Bugattis and vintage sports cars) and Hibernia Auto Restoration, Inc., Hibernia, New Jersey every car is photographed from all possible angles during each stage of dismantling. All parts are tagged as they are removed and stored together. Obviously, this saves much time and mistakes when the car is put back together. Surprisingly, not all of the shops do this. Therefore, it is not naive to ask the owner to describe and show you the methods used to avoid misidentification and loss of parts. A certain amount of order should be apparent. On the other hand, National 1st Prize Winners have come from some rather grimy garages.

Part of the decision will depend on how you and the shop owner get along. If the chemistry is right, he'll agree to do the job and will accept a small deposit to put you "on the list." About a month before he's ready to accept the car he will call you to make the final arrangements. Most shops will request a $500 to $1000 deposit to begin work (usually waived for old customers) and will want you to visit them soon after they receive the car to discuss various details.

A complete restoration can take six months to two years depending on what is involved. A bill is usually rendered once a month and if not paid promptly can result in stoppage of all work and commencement of storage charges or worse. If you have discussed the financial side of the transaction with the shop in a frank and open way, you will not face unexpected surprises.

For many enthusiasts, the ability to pay for the professional restoration of a favorite automobile is the culmination of every secret desire ever held. There is an exhilaration and satisfaction in every dollar spent to put every nut and bolt in its proper place, to see at least one object in this world brought close to perfection. When it's all over, he has the ultimate satisfaction. Utility. He can drive it home.

Chapter 5

Do It Yourself Restoration: Why and How?

Without question, the overwhelming majority of old car restorations are done by the owners. To put it in another way, these cars are not restored by professional restoration shops. Few do-it-yourself restorers do every part of the job themselves but they do take on the responsibility of being the prime contractor. This means all the work revolves around you and it also means a restoration completed at a final cost substantially lower than a professional shop would charge.

Cost savings is not the only motivation involved in deciding on the do-it-yourself route. There is the satisfaction of doing the work yourself, of mastering new skills, and of producing a prize winner with your own skill and knowledge.

A do-it-yourself Model A Ford restoration. Not perfect but perfectly wonderful for fun and (possible) profit. Owner: Ernest Swanson, Ridgefield, Conn.

This does not mean that you will not use professional assistance. It is almost impossible to do every single job involved in a restoration yourself. If your time is limited you can confine yourself to dismantling and reassembling, farming out each part to the specialist needed to restore it and putting it back together when it is returned to you.

Even if you are anxious to do as much of the work as possible you cannot learn every skill required unless you plan to devote a lifetime to the restoration of one car. You will be limited by the amount of money you want to invest in tools. Even professional restoration shops send work out to specialists as it is simply uneconomical to employ specialists in every field required.

The remaining chapters of this book are based on the premise that you will be doing most of the work yourself or, at least, that you will be responsible for seeing that the work is done and done properly. This may be the case even if you are giving the car to a professional shop. Any work you can do or can be responsible for will reduce the bill and most restoration shops are delighted to work on this basis.

A great deal of the time devoted to restoration is drudgery. Removing paint, wire brushing, sanding, cleaning, and polishing are typical examples. A professional restoration shop charges the same price for this work as they do for wiring, fitting, and assembling. If you can do the drudge jobs you can save a great amount of money. Keep track of your hours and calculate the savings at $15 per hour.

Just as important is the time you will spend in locating missing parts. Time spent in this important pursuit can also be calculated as saving $15 per hour as any restoration shop will charge you at approximately this rate for time devoted to "chasing parts."

Chapter 6

How To Begin

Begin with a place to work — where car and tools will remain undisturbed — and a camera. The first thing to do is photograph the car from every possible angle inside and out. Black and white film is fine as it is quicker and less expensive to have 8 by 10 enlargements made. Use a camera that will take quality pictures, at least a good 35mm or, better yet, a larger format camera such as a Rolleiflex. The idea is to produce enlargements that are sharp in every detail. Buy a book especially made to hold 8 by 10 prints under cellophane paper (try your local camera store or photography section of a department store.)

A photographic record of the car before it is taken apart is important for, strangely enough, you will forget how it looked originally. Don't miss the details. Photograph all sides of the engine compartment, the hinges and locks of the hood and trunk and of each door. Don't forget the tops and bottoms of the doors when they are open as well as the top and bottom of the door sills. Pick a working area that is large enough to allow you to work on the body and chassis separately. An area the size of two cars is satisfactory. Be sure there is adequate artificial light as you can expect to work frequently at night. Check the electrical outlets and, if you're in a cold climate, be sure the place is heated or can be heated. With a valuable car and tools on hand you should be certain the building is secure. Paint the inside of the windows and nail up heavy screening on the inside. If the value of your car or cars is more than a few thousand dollars you would do well to look into the possibility of installing an alarm system.

A clean place to work is essential. Scrub the floor with soap and water and paint it light grey to make the dropped parts easier to find. While you're at it, paint the walls and ceiling the same light grey. It will brighten the room and you'll be more inclined to keep the shop clean.

A work bench, tools, and a place to store them, is desirable. Buy used ones through your local "buy-lines," "mart," or newspaper. Don't forget you will need metric tools if you are restoring a car made on the Continent of Europe or British Whitworth tools if the car was made in Great Britain. As a minimum you will need the following to get started:

3 screw drivers: straight edge — small, medium, large.
3 screw drivers: Phillips head — small, medium, large.
Full set of box end wrenches.
Full set of open end wrenches.
Full set of ½" or ⅜" socket wrenches with extension and ratchet bar.
2 Vice Grips: miniature and medium.
1 ballpeen hammer.
1 copper hammer.
1 cold chisel (to knock off bolt heads)
1 8" crescent wrench.
1 electric ⅜" variable speed drill.
1 standard set of high speed drill bits.
1 wire brush head to fit drill.

1 Hacksaw with extra blades.
Wire brushes — soft and hard.
Scrapers — wide and narrow.
1 set of starter punches.
1 set of pin punches (to finish the job).

Don't skimp on tools. A full set of good tools will save you dozens of hours. Keep your hands and tools clean and always use the correct size for the job.

Keep a notebook on the car and its progress. An ordinary hard cover composition book is fine. Use this book for explanations and special notes that are not covered photographically. It will be especially useful to record solutions to parts problems and parts sources. Record keeping will save time in the long run.

Keep track of every penny you spend on the car. Make your entries in the back of the notebook. For a complete record show the date the purchase was made, whom it was paid to, include a description of what it was paid for, and the total amount. A complete financial record can be invaluable in proving how much you spent to a future purchaser or how little you spent — to your wife.

You will find the Yellow Pages of the telephone book extremely useful. Call the business office of your telephone company and request a copy of every Yellow Page directory for every city within 50 miles of your home (100 miles or more if you live far away from any big city.) These directories are usually available free on request.

Chapter 7:
The Art of Dismantling

What could be easier than taking apart a watch? And
what could be more difficult than putting it together?
Taking things apart, willy-nilly, can be terribly destructive
and taking a car apart without following proper procedures
will reduce its value to a fraction of its real worth. The correct method of dismantling is important and here is a list of
some of the rules to be followed:

1) Remove the battery!

2) When removing nuts and bolts and washers to undo
parts, always fasten the nut and bolt and washer back on
to the removed part. If you are removing bolts from a
panel and it is threaded, always screw the bolt back into
the original thread. If you don't follow this procedure you
will end up the coffee cans filled with nuts and bolts with
no idea where they belong. If you must send some items
out for plating, photograph them first and put them in a
plastic bag tagged to indicate where they should go.

3) Before you remove a part, photograph it, showing the
surrounding area to indicate how it is installed. When you
remove the part, place an identifying tag on it.

4) As you remove parts which reveal other parts, photograph each step. Example: The inside of a door.

5) As you remove any part from the car try to imagine yourself putting the same part back six months or a year later. Where an unusual number of steps are involved or where the order in which the items are installed is important, you must keep a record of the correct procedure in your notebook. In some cases, you may find that making drawings of the parts and accompanying notes are needed to reassemble them later. Photograph them also. The drawings and notes will simply explain the photographs. All this photographing and note-taking may seem tedious but you will find it invaluable later as you simply will not be able to remember every detail of the assembly when the time comes to put it all back together.

6) If you are planning a thorough restoration which will result in a prize-winning car, you will want to remove the body and all other parts and start with a bare chassis. Most bodies are attached by six or eight bolts to the frame. Before you can take off the body you must remove the seats, floorboards, and steering column. Then, disconnect all lines running from the chassis to the body. These include:

1) Electric wires — when these are cut, wrap paper tape around each wire to form a tab and mark both ends you have just cut with a code letter or number. Use a different code for each cut.

2) Speedometer and tachometer (if any) cables, oil pressure line from engine to gauge, water temperature line from radiator to gauge, and lines to any other gauges your car may have.

3) If you have hydraulic brakes, drain all the fluid from the system and disconnect the line going from the master cylinder to the brake fluid reservoir tank.

4) If you have vacuum operated windshield wipers you need to remove the vacuum line from the engine.

Remove all fenders, running boards, trim panels on both sides of the engine compartment, radiator shell, and radiator. Photograph the area where the part has been removed, first circling the bolt lines with white chalk for future identification.

Make a further study of the body to be sure nothing more needs to be removed on your particular car. If you are working on a closed car, remove the doors. Check again to be sure you have located and removed all bolts holding the body to the frame.

Now you need four or five strong friends to help you. With two or three on either side it should be possible to lift off the body. If it does not come off, look for bolts you might have missed; otherwise, you may have a rust problem which has bonded the brackets together. Try soaking them in Liquid Wrench and giving each bracket a hard shot with the hammer. If all else fails, you may have to place four jacks under the body and slowly jack the body off the frame, or you may have overlooked some bolts.

With the body off, the chassis should be photographed from all angles before further dismantling takes place. Next, remove the engine, gearbox, and drive shaft separately. Do not proceed further without a Workshop Manual for your car. These are available for most makes and usually give detailed instructions for removal of the rear axle springs, and other suspension parts.

Remove the gas tank and inspect the inside for rust. Even a small amount of rust here can clog fuel lines and flood the carburetors. To remove any rust fill the tank with just enough gravel to cover the bottom. Now find a friend to help you and shake the tank vigorously in all directions. Wash out with water and repeat. When all the rust is removed, let the tank dry and use a fuel tank slushing compound. (We suggest Pro Tech, manufactured by Pro Tech Products Co., 8846 Alondra Blvd., Bellflower, Calif. 90706.) Fill the tank with the slushing compound as directed, tape all holes and rotate the tank in all directions. Blow out the pickup tube after an hour or two and let dry for 24 hours. The tank is now sealed with a rubberlike skin.

By this time the frame should be resting on saw horses or jack stands and you can now remove everything from the frame that is removable. Don't forget to photograph the frame at each stage of removal and tag each part describing its position in the car.

Chapter 8

Engine, Transmission, Rear Axle, Brakes, Suspension, and Steering

Now that you have the car completely dismantled, spread on the floor all around you, it is wise to take an hour or two to decide just how much of this work you want to do yourself. You may be discouraged at the tremendous number of parts that make up a complete automobile. Now is the time to decide which jobs require specialized knowledge which you do not possess and do not wish to acquire.

Engine, Transmission and Rear Axle

These are among the largest and most important parts of the car and do require very special skills, knowledge, and experience to rebuild. If you are restoring a Ford you might ask the Service Manager at your local Ford dealer if any of the older mechanics might be interested in taking on your job on his own time at his house. Regardless of make, you will get the best job done at the lowest price by seeking out a shop or individual mechanic with direct experience in your particular make of car. If you own a very rare car, such as a Bugatti, it is particularly important to entrust it only to a shop specializing in that type of car.

Most professional restoration shops are delighted to carry out a rebuild on your running gear and many of these are able to run the engines before returning them to you. If the shop is not too far away, you will probably prefer to tow the chassis to them, when it is completed, and let them install the engine (and other components) before it is started for the first time.

If you should decide to rebuild the engine and the rest of the running gear yourself, you should obtain a Workshop Manual and the advice and assistance of an experienced mechanic.

Brakes

Bring your brake drums and brake shoes to a local brake shop (look under "Brake Service" in your telephone book Yellow Pages). They will check the inside of the drums for out-of-round wear and will skim them off, if needed, to bring them back to true round. The brake shoes will be lined with new material. A soft lining material is recommended if your car has mechanical brakes or hydraulic brakes with no booster, i.e., without power assist. The softer lining will result in lower pedal pressure and a more progressive braking effect that is easier to control.

Brake fluid is a very effective but expensive paint remover. To avoid any possibility of ruining an expensive paint job you should investigate the newly developed silicone brake fluid which is inert and has no effect on any type of paint. (Contact the Marketing Supervisor, Mechanical Fluids, Dow Corning Corp., Midland, Michigan 48640.) A further benefit of silicone brake fluid is the fact that it does not attract and absorb water as ordinary brake fluid does. This feature alone makes it ideal for old cars whose brake lines, wheel cylinders, and master cylinders are particularly susceptible to corrosion.

Suspension

Springs that are sagging or broken should be replaced. If the springs are sagging you will have to check the workshop manual for the original specifications: take your springs and specifications to your local automotive spring specialist (see Yellow Pages in your telephone book under "Springs-Automotive-Sales and Service").

King pins and bushings should be examined and replaced if excessively worn.

The front spindles, the shafts which hold the brakes and wheels, should be magnafluxed to detect cracks in the metal which might cause the spindle to break. Usually, the local "hot rod" or racing shop will know where the nearest magnaflux service is located. (See your telephone book Yellow Pages under "Automobile Racing and Sports Car Equipment.")

Steering

The steering arm should also be magnafluxed. This is the large part which controls the tie rods and is attached directly to the shaft coming out of the steering box.

An old car which steers badly is unpleasant to drive and is a danger on the roads. Carefully examine every part of the entire steering mechanism and replace all worn or broken parts. The key to good steering is the steering box itself. Take it apart completely and replace all worn bushings and parts that are defective or broken (see your workshop manual for detailed instructions on dismantling, reassembly, and final adjustment to eliminate "play"). Replace worn tie rod ends and ball joints. If you replace or rebuild every worn part from the steering wheel to the front wheels, and if it is all properly adjusted, you will enjoy steering equal to or better than that which the car possessed when new.

Chapter 9:

Rust, Corrosion, Grease, Dirt and Paint Removal

Will Coca-Cola remove rust? Yes, it will and it's worth remembering in a pinch but most uneconomical for any extended use. Take the frame and other large, heavy steel pieces to a sandblasting shop, *after* they have been cleaned with gunk or by steam cleaning. Parts that are excessively dirty and greasy *are* best cleaned by steam cleaning. Professional steam cleaning units can be rented from many large hardware stores. (See "Steam Cleaning Equipment" in your telephone book Yellow Pages.) The sandblasting will remove all rust and paint and all other foreign matter. Do not sandblast any body panels, or any lightweight panels. Immediately the parts are returned from the sandblasters, wash them down with paint thinner to remove all dust, wait for it to dry and paint them with a good enamel or lacquer primer. Fill any corroded areas with "body filler" available from any automotive paint shop. An unusual product which removes rust without sandblasting and creates its own primer surface is "OSPHO" made by Rusticide Products Co., 3125 Perkins Ave., Cleveland, Ohio 44114. "Ospho" painted on a rusted surface that has been wire brushed will turn the iron oxide into iron phosphate, an inert substance that turns the metal black after a white residue is brushed off.

Smaller parts can be derusted and stripped by leaving them for a few hours in a diluted solution of sulphuric acid. A much safer method is to use PF-47 chemical rust remover offered in Appendix III.

Removing paint from large or small sheet metal panels can be handled in several ways. If you don't want to do it yourself try taking the pieces to your local furniture stripper. Their equipment is usually large enough to handle items as large as fenders and doors. For the main structure of the body you will have to use commercial paint remover, purchased by the gallon from your local paint or hardware store. This is hard work and is best done outdoors. The sun will accelerate the process and the foul smell will be blown away. Follow the directions on the can, wear gloves, and move the paint off with wire brushes and steel wool. Wash thoroughly with water and let dry. Then wash again with paint thinner and let dry. Finally, go over all surfaces with a blow torch being careful not to heat the metal so it cannot be touched as overheating will cause the metal to distort. All of these final steps are to eliminate foreign matter which can cause the paint to "lift."

Chapter 10:

Coachwork, Metal Fabricating, Painting, and Striping

If a fender or other panel is rusted or corroded beyond repair you will be facing a tough or easy problem, depending on the type of car involved. Pre-war Ford fenders and most other Ford body parts are available from firms specializing in Ford parts. Fenders for post-war American cars are available from junk yards or thru other collectors and clubs specializing in that make of car. Body parts for very rare and limited production cars such as Rolls Royce and Duesenberg must be *made*.

Coachbuilding, the fabricating of complete automobile bodies in metal involving compound curves, is an almost extinct art in the U.S. Only a handful of the shops listed in Appendix I are capable of producing a complete automobile body and only a few more can make a fender or door. Call the restoration shops nearest to you. If they cannot do the

A new radiator shell for a Ford racer made by metal fabrication specialists. Credit: Chester Auto Restoration Service, Chester N.J.

A better than new professionally painted chassis will be achieved by filling all the low spots with "filler" after the primer has been applied. Credit: Vintage Auto Restorations Inc., Ridgefield, Conn.

job themselves, they will probably be able to refer you to a shop who can.

Metal fabricating that does not involve compound curves is easier to cope with. If nearby restoration shops are not able to assist you try the Yellow Pages of your telephone book under "Assembly and Fabricating," "Metal Stamping" and "Tanks-Metal."

Traditional preference among old car lovers and professional restorers is still for the original pre-war type of lacquer, and it is used in the great majority of fine restorations despite its tendency to crack with age. Aluminum bodied cars are especially prone to paint cracking because aluminum expands and contracts to a greater degree than steel. The lacquer does not expand and contract to the same degree and cracking will eventually result at stress points, e.g., at the corners of the trunk lid where a narrow radius exists.

Enamel expands and contracts more than lacquer. It is generally more flexible and is, therefore, much less prone to cracking. Unfortunately, it is difficult to apply enamel to achieve a perfect result and it is usually too soft to smooth out by the use of fine rubbing compounds such as would be used on a lacquer surface.

The new acrylic automotive paints are just coming into general use in restoration work and are worth serious consideration for their special qualities. Acrylic enamel is ideal for use on aluminum bodied cars as it expands and contracts like ordinary enamel but is much harder and can be rubbed out after allowing a month or two to harden. An ideal acrylic enamel for the beginner to try is DuPont Centari. It dries in air in 20 to 30 minutes provided the humidity in the air is low. Use it with a compatible primer and follow the directions carefully.

Acrylic lacquer will produce a superb glass-like finish but is known to be very hard and difficult to rub out with compound. However, hard work will produce outstanding results and there is every indication that acrylic lacquer will far outlast the ordinary lacquer.

Whatever you use be sure the filler, the primer coat, and the finish coats are all compatible. The use of an enamel

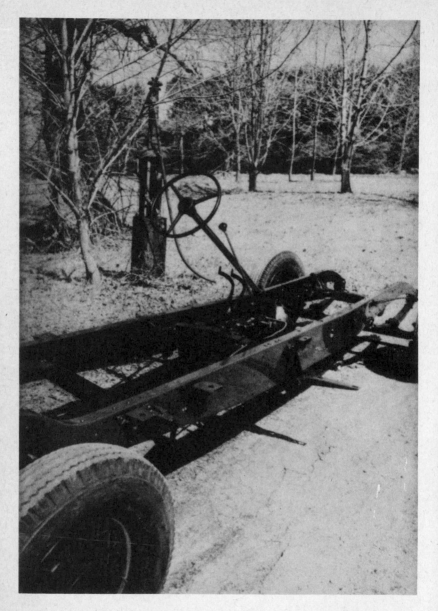

A completed chassis that has been professionally restored to better than new condition. Note the reflections on the side of the frame! Credit: Vintage Auto Restorations Inc., Ridgefield, Conn.

primer with a lacquer finish, for example, will result in the lacquer "lifting" off the surface. Also, for best results, do not paint on days of high humidity or extremely high heat (over 85 degrees).

Striping

Striping machines are available from large hardware stores and art supply stores, but the results they produce are disappointing. The professionals do their striping "free-hand" but unless you have an aptitude for this art you should find a professional to do it for you. If you cannot locate one through the members of your car club try the nearest "hot rod/custom car shop" as striping has become a very popular form of decoration for those types of cars. Also, many sign painters can stripe cars and these can be easily found in the telephone book Yellow Pages.

For post-war cars, try the newly developed clear tape stripes which are applied like scotch tape. These stripes are available in various widths and colors and are quite convincing if you don't examine the surface of the car too closely. (See under "Automobile Parts and Supplies — Retail" in your telephone book Yellow Pages.)

Chapter 11

Road Wheels and Steering Wheels

You may find it less expensive to buy new or rebuilt wheels, road or steering, rather than attempt restoration: see Appendix III for a full list of parts suppliers and wheel restorers.

Road Wheels
Wooden wheels are being made new and repaired by professional wheelwrights. One of the best is Graber and Sons Wheelwrights, 2136 Magnolia Ave., Petaluma, Calif. 94952. Minor repairs can be handled by a local cabinet maker if you can talk him into it.

Metal disc wheels can be repaired and straightened by a wheel shop in the nearest big city. (See under "Wheels" in your telephone book Yellow Pages.)

Wire wheels that are out of round, rusted, cracked, or

An original Model A Ford steering wheel. Owner: Ernest Swanson, Ridgefield, Conn.

A wire wheel in primer after being returned from a specialist rebuilding service. Credit: Vintage Auto Restorations Inc., Ridgefield, Conn.

have broken spokes, must be rebuilt. They must be completely taken apart, sandblasted and made perfectly round with new spokes as required, painted or chrome plated, and balanced. Wire wheels are a specialty and unless a local service exists which will tackle your wheels we recommend you have the work done by Dayton Wheel Products, Inc., 2326 E. River Rd., Dayton, Ohio 45439. To find a possible local shop, call your nearest M.G., Triumph, or Jaguar new car dealer's Service Manager.

Chapter 12:
Tires

What was once a difficult replacement job has been made easy by the tremendous demand created by the ever-increasing number of hobbyists. If the size of your tire was very popular you will find a wide variety of makes and styles available (see Appendix III). If the size you require is not available commercially, advertise for it in a magazine such as *Hemming's* or *Old Cars* (see Appendix III).

The new "old tires and tubes" made now are using modern materials and have all but eliminated the memorable and frequent "blowouts" of the past. This is one part of automotive history we do not want to preserve.

Check your Owner's Manual and be sure to buy the tire size used on your car originally. Do not be tempted by oversized tires which may fit your rims. They will make your car look "tire heavy" and will put a strain on the steering and other running gear it was not originally designed for.

Chapter 13

Platers and Polishers

Some years ago I visited one of the best professional restoration shops in Los Angeles. The owner and I chatted as he prepared a shipment of small parts in a heavy crate. I guessed that these were parts to be chrome plated and I inquired as to why they were being crated. The answer was that all of his plating was done in San Francisco despite the fact that there were over a dozen platers in the Los Angeles area.

The problem is that most platers are not very interested in restoration work and are not sympathetic to the needs of the restorer. Unfortunately, a great many of the items that require plating are badly worn and/or require repairs which most platers cannot cope with. Commercial platers build their business on job lot work that usually consists of plating new parts for a manufacturer on a contract basis. The plating of old worn pieces on an individual basis is usually

This Model A Ford mascot's beauty is due, in large measure, to the fine details in the bird's head, tail and wings. A plater that is not very careful can polish these details away greatly reducing the beauty and value of the mascot. Owner: Ernest Swanson, Ridgefield, Conn.

done as an "accommodation," often with the implication that they are doing you a favor.

A new development is the plater who is specializing in restoration work and who is willing to do some repair work. (See Appendix III.) If one of those shops is not near you and you don't want to do business by mail you might try locating a plater who specializes in marine hardware. (See under "Plating" in your telephone book Yellow Pages.)

Repairs to items made of copper, brass, or aluminum can usually be made by a local silversmith or, for smaller parts, even a jeweler.

Finding someone to repair pitted and/or damaged zinc die castings is even more difficult. One expert in this specialty is Milestone Car Society member Bill Parmenter, 5502 28th Parkway, Hillcrest Heights, Md. 20031, who is setting up a service to help restorers. Alternatively, discuss your problem pieces with the most cooperative plater you can find.

Platers are also professional polishers. Before the plating can begin, the item must be thoroughly cleaned and highly polished. Thus, polishing can be destructive unless the operator is very careful! Thin pieces can be polished through until they disappear. The detail work cast or engraved in a trim piece or sculptured mascot can be polished away. On delicate items like this the plater must be warned to keep his polishing to a minimum.

Polishing of brass lamps and other brightwork is best done the hard way, by hand. Use a good polish such as Brasso and keep the items covered as much as possible to inhibit oxidation.

Inferior plating is useless. All plating on an old car is subject to close scrutiny. Let the plater know that you expect a quality job and that any piece which later blisters or flakes off will be required to be redone properly. Quality plating means plating first with copper, next with nickel and, finally, with chrome. Similar steps are taken with

A record photo made of windshield hardware before the pieces are sent to the platers. A list of the items is also made, matching the photo, and a copy is given to the plater to serve as an inventory. Credit: Vintage Auto Restorations Inc., Ridgefield, Conn.

nickel plating, which was the correct finish before chrome came into general use in the 1930's.

When you pick up work from the plater's be sure to inspect it carefully and immediately return any pieces which show signs of blistering or flaking. Also, watch for areas which have not been fully plated. Sometimes these are deep within a cavity or in a severely under-cut area and the plater may not be able to do any better without special equipment.

Threaded parts (screws, bolts, and studs) that are plated will usually not fit back into their original threaded place (nut or other topped piece) due to the additional thickness of the plating. To avoid this problem ask your plater to mask these parts. If he charges extra for this you can mask them yourself with sealing wax or black plastic electrical tape.

Plating wire or small springs will cause them to become brittle. Heat treating will be required to offset this. If your plater does not know what to do get advice from a heat treating expert. (Look under "Heat Treating — Metal" in your telephone book Yellow Pages.)

Some other forms of plating which may be useful in restoration work can also be recommended:

Cadmium — ideal for rust proofing nuts and bolts.

Soft Chrome — The result is a satin finish not unlike hand polished steel. The finish is sometimes used for front axles, tie rods, and steering arms.

Chapter 14

Woodwork

Woodwork problems fall into three categories: 1) reproduction of wooden parts destroyed by rot or termites, 2) restoration of wooden parts that have deteriorated badly and
may also be partially destroyed, 3) refinishing of metal
parts that were originally woodgrained. The first and last
require special equipment and skill but the second one is
easy to learn and refinishing kits giving excellent results are
available in any hardware store.

Reproduction of Wooden Parts
There are services available to the automotive hobbyist
which will copy wooden pieces using your old piece as a
pattern (see Appendix III). Your local cabinet maker (see
under "Cabinet Maker" in your telephone book Yellow
Pages) is also capable of reproducing these wooden pieces

Woodgraining applied by hand to a window molding by a professional. Credit: Hibernia Auto Restorations Inc., Hibernia, N.J.

if you can talk him into doing it. Again, a visit in a fellow club member's fully restored old car may get him interested enough to help you.

Some wood parts are available immediately from the parts supplier who specializes in your make.

Restoration of Wooden Parts

Refinishing of decorative wood pieces can be accomplished quite easily using materials available in any paint or hardware store. Definitive refinishing instructions can be found in numerous books available in the library. If that's too much trouble, buy a refinishing kit — also available in

A good example of a record shot showing the construction of a wood framed door and how blocks of wood were carefully pieced into the door frame to provide strong new wood for the hinge screws. Credit: Vintage Auto Restorations Inc., Ridgefield, Conn.

paint and hardware stores — and follow the directions to the letter.

Dry Rot in Wood

The bodies of many of the more expensive luxury cars of the pre-World War II and early post-war period were made with hardwood framing to which the aluminum or steel panels were attached. If the wood framing is rotted, you will have to have it all replaced. If it is not rotted, test the wood by inserting the sharp end of a pen knife blade into the wood (with the grain—not across the grain). If the wood is "as new" it will take a great deal of effort to insert the knife. If the knife goes in easily but the wood is otherwise not rotted, the wood can probably be saved by drilling holes ½" apart to 80% of the depth of the wood and pouring in "Git-Rot" (marketed by Boat Life, Hicksville, N.Y. 11801 thru most boat-yards and boat dealers). Follow the directions carefully. This is a plastic substance that is mixed from two different cans. This substance will restore the strength of dry rotted wood provided the wood is not rotted so badly that it is falling apart. It is particularly important to use this treatment where door hinges are screwed into the wood and at joints where two pieces of wood are joined.

Restoration of Wood Grained Metal Parts

Kits are available and you can learn to do this yourself. At slight additional cost and great reduction in frustration we recommend having woodgraining done professionally (see Appendix III).

Chapter 15

Springs: Large and Small

Large coil springs and leaf springs used for the suspension of a car are available from the nearest automotive spring shop (see "Springs — Automotive — Sales and Service" in your telephone book Yellow Pages). If the original specifications for the springs are available, bring them along with the springs from the car. Final adjustment, shimming or re-arching, cannot be done until the car is completely reassembled with all of its weight again on the chassis.

Small springs are available in almost infinite variety from a spring supply house (see "Springs — Coil, Flat, etc. — Distrs. and Mfrs." in your telephone book Yellow Pages). Special springs can be made to order. The usual minimum order is one to two dozen so you may want to pool your order with other club members to make it worthwhile. Be sure

This chrome plated spring steel bumper for a Model A Ford is available from Ford parts specialists but this type of bumper can be made by an automotive spring shop. Owner: Ernest Swanson, Ridgefield, Conn.

to bring a sample and make it clear that you want precisely the same design. Also, be sure to specify that the diameter and strength of the wire must be the same as the sample.

If small springs must be chrome plated be sure they are heat treated to take away the brittleness (see Chapter 13).

With dimensioned drawings, or from an old set of original springs, an automotive spring shop can duplicate this quarter-elliptic spring from a Type 51A Bugatti. Credit: Vintage Auto Restorations Inc., Ridgefield, Conn.

This headlight shell can be made by the metal spinning process. The smaller parts would be added later by a metal fabricator. Credit: Vintage Auto Restorations Inc., Ridgefield, Conn.

Chapter 16:
Spun Metal Parts

Large, hollow, symmetrical pieces, e.g., headlight rims and shells, are easily reproduced by a process known as metal spinning. In metal spinning, a thin sheet of steel, aluminum, copper, or brass is shaped over a wooden mold which is the exact shape and size of the piece you wish to reproduce. First, locate a metal spinner. This could be a small local company in the metal spinning business (see under "Metal Spinning" in the telephone book Yellow Pages), or the metal working teacher in the local high school. A company may require a minimum order of a dozen or more. In this case, spread the word in your car club and take orders for the extra pieces you can't use.

Chapter 17:
Cast Metal Parts

Any cast metal part can be reproduced by a foundry. Small foundries usually work in aluminum, brass, and bronze alloys. In most cases, only larger foundries will cast iron or steel and they are usually not interested in doing small jobs for hobbyists. Don't worry. There are dozens of items you can have made easily and inexpensively by a small foundry. A partial list: door handles (inside and out), window winding handles, metal knobs, metal pull handles, mascots, hub covers, engine mounts, valve covers, and water jacket plates. (See under "Foundries" in your telephone book Yellow Pages.)

If you give an original piece to the foundry to use as their

Chapter 18:
Machined Parts

Small fully-machined parts can be reproduced from the original or from drawings by any competent machinist. Here again, the problem is to find the right machinist and/or the right machine shop (See under "Automobile Machine Shop Service" and "Machine Shops" in your telephone book Yellow Pages.) You might also try finding a part-time or retired machinist by advertising in the local Help Wanted columns.

A Ford Model A rumble seat step plate which could be made by a machine shop if it were not available from a Ford parts specialist. Owner: Ernest Swanson, Ridgefield, Conn.

This knurled knob is a typical machine shop item which can be very expensive if only one is made or quite inexpensive if made in quantity. Owner: Ernest Swanson, Ridgefield, Conn.

Chapter 19:

Glass, Plexiglas and Plastics

Glass parts cannot be reproduced economically in small quantities. Many glass parts are available commercially, "NOS" or reproductions, and a thorough search of these sources is advised before you investigate the possibility of making new parts. Any commercial glass company will want a minimum order of 500 to 1,000 pieces representing a sizable investment. If your club is interested in such a project, look for a likely glass company in the telephone book Yellow Pages of the nearest large city under the section "Glassware — Whol. & Mfrs."

Small glass pieces can be reproduced with convincing results in clear or colored plastic. Only close examination will reveal they are not real glass. This method of reproduction is done by the rubber mold method previously described in Chapter 17. Small plastic pieces can be reproduced the same way. (See under "Plastics — Molders" in the telephone book Yellow Pages.)

Flat safety glass for windshields, side, and rear windows is easily obtained from your local automotive glass shop. (See under "Glass — Automobile, Plate, Window, Etc. —

Small lenses that were originally made in glass can be economically reproduced in small quantities in plastic by the rubber mold method. Owner: Ernest Swanson, Ridgefield, Conn.

Dealers" in your telephone book Yellow Pages.) When having windshield glass replaced, be sure state inspection laws are met. In most states the glass must be specially marked to show it is approved safety glass.

Curved safety glass for the windshield is more difficult. Owners of old Ferrari's have located several sources for custom made curved safety glass and I suggest you write to both the Ferrari Owner's Club and the Ferrari Club of America (See Appendix II) for the latest information on this subject.

For curved rear windows or side windows, install Plexiglas. Specialists in bending and installing Plexiglas can usually be found through automobile racing shops and also at airport shops specializing in airplane and helicopter interiors. Or you can try cutting, forming, and fitting it yourself. Suggestions are available from Plexiglas suppliers found under "Plastics — Rods, Tubes, Sheets, Etc. — Supply Centers" in the telephone book Yellow Pages.

Chapter 20

Broken Pieces: Welding and Metal Stitching

Using the techniques of industry in the area of "cold welding," hot welding and metal stitching, it is possible to repair almost anything that has been broken. Even in cases of an engine destroying itself by "throwing a rod" it is usually possible to repair the engine to its original running condition. Every restoration shop which does engine work must know the techniques in current use and have the ability to carry out these repairs themselves or have experience with specialists who can be trusted.

The welding of large aluminum castings such as cylinder heads is probably the most difficult repair to effect with 100% success. Welding aluminum can cause it to distort so it will no longer fit the piece it is to be mated to. The answer is Heli-Arc welding, a low temperature gas weld in an atmosphere of helium. Using this method an experienced

An excellent example of metal stitching. In this case, a hole in the side of a engine block is replaced with a steel plate that is stitched to the block by the use of interlocking threaded brass plugs. This is a "cold" process which precludes the possibility of distortion. Credit: Vintage Auto Restorations Inc., Ridgefield, Conn.

operator can make the repair with no measurable distortion.

Acetylene gas welding can be used to repair successfully iron blocks and other cast iron pieces and distortion will not be measurable provided the area to be welded is not too large. For large areas metal stitching is much less risky. This method is completely cold. Holes are drilled between the original block and the repair plate. The holes are tapped and brass plugs threaded in so they overlap and interlock. This method guarantees no distortion.

If distortion does occur in a piece that has been welded it can be corrected by remachining one or more of the surfaces. Expensive but not a total disaster.

Chapter 21

Instruments and Electrical System

Instruments

The restoration of instruments can require four separate operations:

1) The nickel or chrome plating, or polishing, or painting of the rim surrounding the face.

2) Renewing of the face. In some cases only careful cleaning is required. In others, the face is so faded or chipped or discolored that it is hardly legible and a new face must be made exactly duplicating the original.

3) The instrument works should be sent out to a competent instrument repair man even if you know the instrument is working properly. This is done to be sure the instrument is clean, properly lubricated, that all connections are tight, and that no part is so worn that it is about to fail.

This full set of original instruments on a 1928 Bentley 4 ½ litre LeMans Tourer are in very good original condition and are preferable to a new reproduction.

4) The back of the case must be derusted and cleaned and painted.

Several services are listed in Appendix III which will take care of all these services and return the instrument to you in "as new" condition.

If you want to handle these operations separately, do not take the instrument apart. Simply clean the outside thoroughly and send it first to an instrument repair service (See Appendix III). When it is returned you can simply paint the back, send the rim to the plater, and the face to a service specializing in this type of work.

If the indicator needle does not come off easily, take it to your nearest watch repair man. He will be able to remove it correctly with his special tools. If necessary, remove the paint from the needle and repaint it with a thin coat of black lacquer applied with a fine brush.

Every detail of this 1938 Delahaye instrument panel has been professionally restored. Credit: Vintage Auto Restorations Inc., Ridgefield, Conn.

Making new faces is part of the normal business of restoring old clocks. Look for a shop near you that sells and/or restores old clocks. They will do the job for you or will be able to refer you to a special service.

If you find that new or rebuilt instruments are available from one of the parts suppliers (See Appendix III) you may save money by buying them rather than having them restored.

Electrical System

Start with a new battery of the correct size. As you will not use the car every day buy a quality battery that will more likely hold its charge for long periods. Also, buy a new ground wire (from the battery to the chassis) and a new "hot cable" (from the battery to the starter motor). A wiring diagram is essential in order to allow duplication of the original electrical system and to enable you to double check your work. Look at the wiring diagram to find out if your system is "positive ground" or "negative ground." If the diagram indicates the ground wire goes from the + (plus) terminal of the battery, you have a positive ground system. If the ground wire goes from the - (minus) terminal, you have a negative ground system. Most old American and English cars are "positive ground" and most old French, German, Swedish, and Italian cars are "negative ground."

Send your starter motor and generator out to be checked and rebuilt as necessary (See "Automobile Electric Service" in your telephone book Yellow Pages.) Paint them when they are returned, being careful not to get the paint into the insides. Also, have them check your voltage regulator. If any of these units require major repairs you may find it cheaper to buy new or rebuilt units from one of the parts suppliers specializing in your type of car.

Replacing every wire in your car can be a tedious and time-consuming project. Fortunately, complete wiring harnesses (all of the wires correctly assembled and wrapped for installation exactly as they were installed by the factory) are available for many of the most popular cars (See Appendix III.)

Check the electrical connections of all the tail lights, head lights, parking lights, brake lights, instrument lights, and interior lights. If any connection is broken and you cannot repair it, try taking it to your local "fixit" man who repairs toasters, waffle irons, etc.

To learn the basic principles of electricity and of your automotive electrical system, consult your local library and the book sellers listed in Appendix III.

Chapter 22:
Upholstery

Under the broad category of upholstery are seats, head-lining, doors, carpet, tops, top boots (tonneau covers), wheel covers, and anything that is made of cloth, leather, or material of any kind.

If your wife or a good friend is a competent seamstress you may be able to get all the upholstery done at a very low cost. However, a normal sewing machine cannot be used to sew upholstery. A heavy duty machine made expressly for heavy materials is required. Books on automotive uphol-stery are available and will be a great help (See Appendix III). Unless you expect to restore a good many cars you will find it less costly to have the work done by an upholsterer than to invest in a heavy duty sewing machine.

For the most popular cars, Fords, M.G.'s, and many others, the favorite solution is the use of upholstery kits.

The top and upholstery of this 1931 Model A Ford kits! Owner: Ernest Swanson, Ridgefield, Conn were made from readily available upholstery

An upholstery kit was used in restoring the seats of this Model A Ford rumble seat. Owner: Ernest Swanson, Ridgefield, Conn.

Most of these kits are of high quality, using the correct original materials. They are easy to install and give a most professional result. Upholstery kits are available for seats, headlinings, tops, panels and trim, side curtains, and top boots (tonneau covers). (See Appendix III)

For the very best work, use a professional upholsterer who specializes in restoration work and who has a reputation for quality work among the members of your club. This type of work is expensive and if you are willing to entrust your work to a less experienced upholsterer you may save a bit. (See "Automobile Seat Covers, Tops & Upholstery" in your telephone book Yellow Pages). An upholsterer with no experience in restoration work will have to be "educated." He must understand that the construction of the upholstery must be *exactly* like the original. Let him know that "short cuts" will not be acceptable. Then tell him that you will not hold him to a fixed estimate in advance, that you will pay him fairly based on the time he spends on the job. Most

Cloth upholstery being professionally installed on a Model A Ford sedan. Credit: Hibernia Auto Restorations, Inc., Hibernia, N.J.

likely this type of upholsterer will not have the correct materials as used on your car originally. You will have to buy the correct materials after he tells you the number of yards he will require for each part.

Again, reconsider the more expensive professional restoration upholsterer. He may be more satisfactory in the long run. He will have the correct materials or will get them. He will guarantee a perfect professional job. You will not have to supervise him each step of the way.

Chapter 23

Preparing For Show

The most important event in the hobby of car collecting is the vast Hershey Show, held in October of each year at Hershey, Pennsylvania by the Antique Automobile Club of America. It is the largest show held in America and most experts consider it the best run, boasting the most objective standards of judging in the hobby. The A.A.C.A. judging procedure leaves little or no room for a judge to be influenced by his own personal likes and dislikes. The procedure in other clubs is not always as fair and personal favoritism of a particular judge can sometimes ruin an otherwise delightful meet. Discuss this subject with the more experienced members of your club. In most clubs this is not a problem but even when it is a problem it can usually be solved by joint action by the members.

To compete successfully you must *know the rules!* Ask

your club for a copy of their "Judging Form" and "Official Judging Manual." A thorough understanding of these documents will give you the best chance to take a First Prize.

The "perfect" car is one that is in precisely the same dondition as it was when it left the factory as a new car. Therefore judging for show is based on the authenticity, workmanship, and maintenance of each component. Although the car must be driven on to the show grounds, no further detailed check of its mechanical condition will be made. A copy of the A.A.C.A. Judging Form is reproduced here and the following is part of the instructions to the judges about the use of this form (under the A.A.C.A. system a perfect score is 400):

"The correct procedure for use of this form is to first inspect the vehicle. When a fault is found, look for the component under consideration on the form and enter the number of points to be deducted in the approporiate block. Judge each component for authenticity, workmanship and maintenance. Deduct the maximum points indicated for non-authentic or missing components. Do not deduct more than the maximum points indicated for any single listed item. When there is multiple use of a component such as doors, lights and wheels, the indicated deduction may be taken for each individual part (Example: If a vehicle has four non-authentic wheels, the deduction is four times the three point maximum deduction for a single wheel, or twelve points total). When judging condition of finish of any component, deduct points for faults such as alighment of components, depth of finish, runs, orange peel, rust, dents, scratches, cracks, lack of paint, lack of plating, etc. Plating must be of the authentic type for the vehicle being judged. Chrome plating prior to 1928 is improper unless authenticity can be documented by the owner (Hard Nickel is not considered a deductible feature). Deduct one point for each component with non-authentic plating, with a maximum deduction of ten points per vehicle for non-authentic plating. Do not deduct points for slight defects which may have been caused en route to the meet. For example, minor scratches, dents, grease, oil and dirt which obviously are new."

MEET: _____ ENTRY No.: _____ OWNER: _____ MAKE: _____ YEAR: _____ CLASS: _____

EXTERIOR

EXTERIOR	MAX	DED
Body: Door	5	
Fender	5	
Hood	5	
Panel	5	
Trim/Striping	3	
Light: Head	5	
Side	3	
Tail	3	
Driving	3	
Radiator: Shell	5	
Grill	5	
Ornament	3	
Top (Hard)	5	
Horn	3	
Mirror	3	
Windshield Frame	3	
Wind. Wiper	3	
Door Handle	2	
Running Board	5	
Splash Apron	5	
Gas Gen./Tank	3	
Beading/Welting	3	
Incorrect: Body	⑳	
Material	⑮	
Color	⑩	
Other:		
TOTAL DEDUCTION		

INTERIOR

INTERIOR	MAX	DED
Top (Soft):	–	
Missing (Ironed)	⑳	
Down	⑩	
Material	10	
Trim	3	
Fastener	1*	
Top Iron/Bow	3	
Side Curtain	2	
(Missing)	⑩	
Headliner	5	
Seat Cushion/Back	5	
Side Panel	3	
Door Panel	5	
Window Frame	3	
Door Sill	3	
Floor Cover (Mat)	3	
Steering Wheel	3	
Pedal/Lever	2	
Dashboard	3	
Instrument	5	
Foot Rest	5	
Tonneau Wind.	5	
Glass	3	
Trim	3	
Incr. Uphol. Mat'l.	⑩	
Other:		
TOTAL DEDUCTION		

CHASSIS

CHASSIS	MAX	DED
Axle: Front	5	
Rear	5	
Trans/Drive Line	5	
Snubber/Shock	3	
Gas Tank	3	
Steering Assembly	5	
Pow. Steering (Add)	⑩	
Brake	3	
Body Bolt	1*	
Lube Fitting	1*	
Lack of Lube	1	
Excess Lube	1	
Exhaust System	5	
Tire	3	
Wheel	3	
Rim	2	
Lock Ring	1	
Hub Cap	3	
Valve: Stem	1	
Cover	1	
Spring	3	
Spring Cover	2	
Frame	5	
Bumper	5	
Overdrive (Add)	⑩	
Tire Carrier/Cover	3	
Other:		
TOTAL DEDUCTION		

ENGINE

ENGINE	MAX	DED
Block	5	
Head	5	
Crankcase	5	
Manifold	5	
Radiator Core	10	
Starter	5	
Starter (Add)	⑩	
Generator	5	
Fuel Supply	5	
Fuel Supply (Add)	⑩	
Carburetor	5	
Magneto/Dist.	5	
Coil/Horn	3	
Clamp	1*	
Belt	2	
Firewall	3	
Priming Cup	1	
Waterpump	5	
Terminal	1*	
Splash Pan	3	
Wiring	3	
Tape/Tubing	1	
Filter/Fan	3	
Incorrect Engine	⑳	
Ov'hd. Valves (Add)	⑩	
Gauge/Control	3	
Other:		
TOTAL DEDUCTION		

SUMMARY

AWARD

- Junior 1st
- 2nd
- 3rd
- Multiple Award

DEDUCTIONS

- Exterior –
- Interior –
- Chassis –
- Engine –
- TOTAL –

SCORE

Perfect Score	400
Total Deductions	
NET SCORE	

REQUIRED MINIMUM POINTS

1st – 365, 2nd – 330, 3rd – 295

(Multiple awards for scores within 10 points of highest scoring car in each award.)

APPROVED

_____ TEAM CAPTAIN

_____ DEPUTY JUDGE

_____ DEPUTY JUDGE

In their Judging Manual the A.A.C.A. takes up the subject of "over restoration": "Recently there has been much comment, some unfavorable, on the subject of over restoration. From a subjective standpoint this may be commendable but it greatly complicates the problem of judging. The over restored car should not be given any preference over other cars and should be scored according to its appearance as it left the factory." Find out how your own club feels about over restoration before you go too far with your own restoration.

Once your car is restored, preparing for show is simply a meticulous clean up job covering every part of the car. If you use your car quite often the job will take much longer than if you keep the car exclusively for show occasions. The ultimate in this approach are those who keep their car in a heated garage wrapped in a custom made car cover and bring it to a meet in an enclosed trailer! Preparation for these people is usually limited to a thorough dusting of the car and repolishing of the bright work.

For most of us preparation for a show means hard work for several days with a vast array of waxes, polishes, preservatives, stain removers, grease cutters and solvents. Most of these are available from any well stocked hardware or automotive supply store. A few products are worth special mention. One is "Armor All," a liquid which preserves rubber and alleges to prevent the fine cracking usually found on old tires or anything else made of rubber. It also cleans the rubber and gives it that "as new" look. (Armor All is made by Very Important Products, Newport Beach, Ca. 92660.) Another good one is "Lexol" which softens and preserves leather and is available in most hardware stores.

Chapter 24:
Preparing For Storage

First of all you must accept the fact that extended storage is destructive. In the normal course of time, even in a heated garage, engines will seize, metals will rust and corrode, paint will oxidize, gaskets will dry out, gasoline and oil will turn to gum, and within two or three years the car may require a complete rebuild!

By the following specific procedures, the process of destruction can be greatly slowed or completely stopped, but only on a year to year basis. There is no method of preservation which will preserve a car indefinitely.

Certain precautions must be taken regardless of the number of months or years you intend to leave the car in storage. The following rules are basic precautions to be observed:

1) Store the car in a dry garage. If you live in a cold cli-

mate the garage should be heated.

2) Change the oil and refill with a light-weight oil such as 20 weight.

3) Remove the spark plugs, fill with oil and replace the spark plugs.

4) Drain the cooling system and refill with anti-freeze and rust inhibitor. For cars that have well-worn engines, use an alcohol base anti-freeze. The permanent type anti-freezes tend to find minute holes which can create leaks.

5) Cover the air inlet on the carburetors and the end of the exhaust pipe. This is easily done with doubled over plastic sheet and electric tape.

6) Remove the battery and store it in a warm place. Do not store a battery on a concrete floor.

7) Thoroughly wax all painted and plated surfaces.

8) Buy 4 jack stands to place under either side of the rear axle and the front frame members to hold the car off the ground.

9) Keep a dust cover over the car and leave it loose to allow air to circulate underneath.

10) Keep the clutch pedal depressed by wedging a 2" x 4" piece of wood the right length wedged between the clutch pedal and the bottom of the driver's seat, or wedge the clutch pedal open from the engine side of the firewall. In either case this will prevent the clutch plate from adhering to the flywheel due to a build-up of humidity.

For short-term storage, less than one year, leave the car "wet," i.e., the cooling system full of water and anti-freeze, the engine full of oil, and the gas tank full. This will prevent the drying out of gaskets and seals. However, to keep the carburetor from gumming up you must run the engine at least once a month for about thirty minutes to bring the engine up to full operating temperature.

If you will not be able to start the car once a month you should prepare it with very little gas left in the tank, run it until all of the gas is used up (this will clear the carburetors of gas) and *then* fill the gas tank full. This will prevent the formation of corrosion in the gas tank.

Chapter 25

Preparing After Storage

Starting a car after a long period of storage involves a series of prudent precautions and a certain element of luck. I have seen cars started after many years of storage with only a fresh battery, a set of jumper cables and a small can of gasoline.

If you have the facilities available it is prudent to follow a few simple rules to avoid damaging the engine:

1) Establish that the engine is "free," i.e., that the crankshaft, rods, and pistons are free to move. This can be checked by removing the spark plugs and turning the engine by means of a crank or by placing the transmission in 1st gear or Reverse and rocking the car back and forth. If the engine is not "free" add penetrating oil through the spark plug holes and try again. If this doesn't work the engine should be taken apart and rebuilt.

2) Drain the oil and look for pieces of babbit. If you find any don't start the engine. Again, an engine rebuild is indicated. Otherwise, refill with fresh oil.

3) Drain the gas tank. Flush and refill with fresh gas.

4) Charge the battery or, better yet, install a new fully-charged battery.

5) Open the distributor and check the points. If they are pitted, file them even.

6) Clean the spark plugs or replace them with new spark plugs.

7) You are now ready to start the engine. First, engage the starter to turn over the engine with the ignition off. Watch the oil pressure gauge and keep the engine turning until oil pressure is indicated. Now, prime the carburetors with a few tablespoons of gas and try to start the engine with the ignition on. Be sure the choke control is operating freely. If you flood the carburetors, press the accelerator pedal all the way to the floor and try again.

8) If the engine will not start check to be sure that gas is reaching the carburetors. If not, you may have to rebuild the fuel pump. Also, check that electric current is reaching the spark plugs by holding a plug lead very close to the spark plug. If there is no spark, check the ground wire and the hot wire to the coil to be sure all connections are tight. You may require a new coil and/or condenser but at this point you should get an experienced mechanic to assist you.

9) If the engine does start, let it run for at least 30 minutes before attempting to drive it. This will allow the engine to thoroughly warm up and every part will be lubricated.

Postscript

Those of us who have spent many years in restoration work understand only too well that "Murphy's Law" is usually in full operation. "Murphy's Law" is simply that "If anything can go wrong, it will."

Ken Painter of the Maserati Club has stated the case very well and I can do no better than to quote him:

"I list below some of the grim facts about restoration work that I have learned the hard way over the years. These gems contain no mechanical secrets, no short cuts to success; on the contrary, they go a long way towards explaining why you will never succeed in completing your restoration as quickly or as economically as you had expected:

1. If anything can go wrong, it will.
2. Interchangeable parts won't.
3. Any wire or tube cut to length will be too short.
4. Availability of a part is inversely proportional to your need for it.
5. Tolerances will accumulate unidirectionally towards

maximum difficulty of assembly.

6. After a part has been fully assembled, extra components will be found on the bench.

7. A dropped tool will land where it can do most damage, or where it will be most inaccessible. Sometimes it will do both. (This is known as the law of selective gravitation.)

8. Components that must not and cannot be assembled incorrectly, will be.

9. Any error that can creep in, will. It will be in the direction that will do most damage.

10. All constants are variable.

11. The most logical way to assemble a part will be the wrong way.

12. Dimensions will always be expressed in the least usable terms.

13. If a part can be installed incorrectly, that is what you will do.

14. An adjustable spanner used to remove a component will either be too tight or too slack to replace the same part, even if you try to replace it immediately.

15. Hermetic seals will leak.

16. After the last 16 screws are removed from a component, you will find that you are dismantling the wrong part.

17. To estimate the time a restoration will take, carefully work out how long you expect the job to take, then treble it. To estimate the cost, carefully work out all known expenditure, then quadruple it. You will still be wrong, but not as wrong as you would have been if you had believed your first estimates.

Of course, you won't always find that the first 16 of these rules will apply at the same time, Rule 17 operates constantly though. Even so, it can be postulated as Rule 18 that a random percentage will constantly be operating to your disadvantage.

If you still feel that the restoration game is worth a try, then all I can suggest is a visit to your doctor, he will be able to arrange a suitable specialist appointment for you. Whatever you do, don't come to me for help. You see, I've just bought a lovely 3500 GT, but it has a broken gearbox ....."

Appendix I:

Restoration Shops in the U.S. and Canada

ALABAMA
> **Automobile Restoration Co.**
> Rt. 2, Box 285-X
> Wetumpka, Ala. 36092
> 205-567-8974
> **Lonsdale & Young**
> 2323 W. Fairview Ave.
> Montgomery, Ala. 36108
> 205-263-2498
>> MANAGER: John Griffin. Specializes in antiques and classics. Did Bugatti Royale for Mills Lane.

ARIZONA
> **Franklin Service Co.**
> 1405 E. Kleindale Road
> Tucson, Ariz. 85719
> 602-326-8038
>> OWNER: Thomas H. Hubbard. Specializes in classic era Franklins. Restores for Harrah.

CALIFORNIA
> **Andrews Auto Restoration Center**
> 4921 Folsom Blvd.
> Sacramento, Cal. 95819
> 916-452-8127
>> OWNER: Phil H. Andrews. Specializes in complete restoration of classic and special interest cars.
>
> **Bill's Antique Body Works**
> 908 9th Street
> Turlock, Cal. 95380
> 209-634-7996
>> OWNER: William A. Borba.

Coachcraft
8679 Melrose
Los Angeles, Cal. 90069

Custom Auto Service
302 French Street
Santa Ana, Cal. 92701
714-543-2980
    Specialize in classic and postwar Packards. Various hourly rates.

Doug's Auto Body
37 Duffy Place
San Rafael, Cal. 94901
    OWNER: Douglas Shaffer. Complete restoration of antique and classic cars.

Franklin Automobile Restorations
2993 Las Vellis Drive
Thousand Oaks, Cal. 91360
805-497-4417
    OWNER: Tony Giaimo. Specialize in classics.

Mike Goodman's Sport Car Service
14540 Erwin Street
Van Nuys, Cal. 91401
213-780-5052
    MGR: Mike Goodman.

Graber & Sons Wheelwrights
2136 Magnolia Avenue
Petaluma, Cal. 94952
707-763-6217
    OWNER: Ray Graber. Specializes in restoring, rebuilding and duplicating antique and vintage bodies and wooden wheel building and auto woodwork in general.

William H. Lauver
140 South "B" Street
Tustin, Cal. 92680

L & M Auto
11562 Santa Monica Blvd.
Los Angeles, Cal. 90025

Nethercutt Laboratories
15180 Bledsoe Street
Sylmar, Cal. 91342
    OWNER: Jack B. Nethercutt.

Mr. O. A. "Bunny" Phillips
8724 E. Garvey Avenue
So. San Gabriel, Cal. 01777
    Specializes in complete restoration of Bugattis.

Gene Sherman
501 W. Maple Avenue
Orange, Cal. 92666

COLORADO
Antique Auto House, Inc.
3329 No. Garfield
Loveland, Colo. 80537

303-667-7040
        OWNER: John R. Bergquist. Will restore antiques and classics.

CONNECTICUT

Fine Car Engineering Studios
108 N. Main St.
Wallingford, Conn.
203-265-2808
        Full restoration, maintenance, repair, parts, fabrication, body work: lead, fiberglass, lacquer, art work, wood & leather.

Hoe Sportcar
446 Newtown Turnpike
Weston, Conn. 06880
203-227-6462
        OWNER: Jim Hoe. Specializes in mechanical restoration of Duesenbergs and other antiques and classics.

Reuter's Coachworks, Inc.
27R Catoonah Street
Ridgefield, Conn. 06877
203-438-6417
        OWNER: Gus Reuter. No mechanical work. Specializes in restoration of great antique and classic cars.

Vintage Auto Restorations, Inc.
Box 83
Ridgefield, Conn. 06877
203-438-4946
        MGR: Don Lefferts. Specializes in complete mechanical restoration of Bugattis and antique and vintage high performance cars.

FLORIDA

Antique Autos of America
12087 62nd St. N.
Largo, Fla. 33541
813-535-1567

Auto Rebuilding and Restoration Services, Inc.
P.O. Box 96
Florahome, Fla. 32635
904-659-2163
        Complete or partial restorations on any antique or classic; specializing in Model As.

Belote's Antique & Classic Car Garage
949 Broadway
Dunedin, Fla. 33528
813-733-7350
        MGR: Philip W. Belote.

Hayden's Auto Service
4824 Kennedy Road
Tampa, Fla. 33609
813-884-3312
        Antique and classic restorations. Did Millard Newman's 1910 Rolls-Royce Silver Ghost

Horseless Carriage Shop
1881 Main Street (Highway 580)
Dunedin, Fla. 33528
813-733-9340
        MGR: Edward "Bud" Josey.

INDIANA
Custom Trim
1332 W. Main
Ft. Wayne, Ind. 46808
219-422-1633
Custom automotive interiors; classics, antiques, customs.

KANSAS
Pearson Restorations
1511 So. 25th Street
Kansas City, Kan. 66106
OWNER: Jim Pearson. Specializes in classic Rolls-Royces and Cadillacs.

KENTUCKY
Motor Parts Depot, Inc.
211 E. College
Louisville, Ky. 40203

Pearson & Marzian, Inc.
501 E. St. Catherine St.
Louisville, Ky. 40204

Top Brass, Inc.
637 Baxter Avenue
Louisville, Ky. 40204
502-587-7963
MGR: John H. Caperton.

MASSACHUSETTS
The Antique Auto House
P.O. Box 79
Hanover, Mass. 02339
617-878-9861
OWNER: Andrew B. Damon. Does complete restorations of antiques, classic and special interest cars.

Dearborn Automobile Co.
14H Pond St.
Marblehead, Mass. 01945
617-631-3727
Service and restoration of 1950 61 Mercedes-Benz; also, buy, sell, locate.

Moineau Car Co.
419A Lincoln St.
Marlboro, Mass. 01752
617-481-6585
Complete restoration work.

River Street Motors
c/o John Ayoub
106 River St.
Dedham, Mass. 02026
617-329-2480
Restoration of antique, classic and special interest autos, semi- or complete.

Vetco
East & Warwick
Northfield, Mass. 01360
413-498-2627

MGR: Wes Ives. Complete restoration of antique and classic cars.

MICHIGAN

Auto Restorations Inc.
441 Elmwood
Troy, Mich. 48084
313-588-8383

Clark-Patton, Inc.
4775 Curtis
Plymouth, Mich. 48170
313-662-9033
MGR: T. Terry Patton. Restoration of antique and classic cars.

Leonard A. Davis
1345 Whitney Drive
Watkins Lake
Pontiac, Mich. 48054
Specializes in brass era antiques

Fleet Supply Co.
2896 Central Avenue
Detroit, Mich. 48209
313-843-2200
MGR: Walter J. Heater. Complete restoration of antiques.

Andy Hotton Assoc.
510 Savage Road
Belleville, Mich. 48111
313-697-7129
MGR: Donold J. Hotton. Specializes in Ford products only; includes Lincolns.

Jerry Kiefer
33711 Edmonton
Farmington, Mich. 48024
Specializes in classic cars.

Ted Ongena
2145 S. Lapeer Road
Lapeer, Mich. 48446
Specializes in antiques.

Restoration Service
37040 Huron River Drive
New Boston, Mich. 48164
MGR: Fred Witt.

MINNESOTA

Johnson Iron & Machine Co.
P.O. Box 435
1201 De Mers Avenue
East Grand Forks, Minn. 56721
218-773-0525
OWNER: Melvin Johnson. Specializes in antiques.

MISSOURI

Auto of Yesteryear Car Museum & Restoration Shop
Interstate 44 & U.S. 63
Rolla, Mo. 65401
314-364-1810

NEVADA

Adams Custom Engines, Inc.
806 Glendale Avenue
Sparks (East Reno), Nev. 89431
702-358-8070
OWNER/MGR: Everett J. Adams. Does complete restorations of antiques & classics.

Ken Gooding
1150 Marietta Way
Sparks, Nev. 89431
Complete restorations of antique, classic and special interest cars.

James Gullihur
P.O. Box 345
Fernley, Nev. 89408
Complete restoration of antique, classic and special interest cars.

NEW JERSEY

Antique Auto, Inc.
Northfield, N.J. 08225

Antique Auto Shop, Inc.
R.D. #2
Box 281 A
Pleasantville, N.J. 08232
609-927-8729
OWNER: Ralph T. Buckley. Specializes in complete restoration of Simplex Mercer and other antique and classic cars.

Robert J. Gassaway, Inc.
519 Main Street
South Amboy, N.J. 08879
201-721-2260

Henry's Antique Car Shop
174 Somers Landing Road
Oceanville, N.J. 08231
609-641-5873
OWNER: Henry Heinsohn.

Hibernia Auto Restorations, Inc.
Maple Terrace
Hibernia, N.J. 07960
201-627-1882
MGR: Robert E. Turnquist. Complete restorations of all antique, classic and special interest cars.

Hulico-Layton Garage
Doug Hull
Box 78
Layton, N.J. 07851
201-948-4380
Antique auto restorations; metal repair, fabrication, painting, pin striping.

The Restoration Shop
R.D. 1, Box 228
Jamesburg, N.J. 08831
201-521-1128
Owner: Earl Lewis. Twenty-one national first prize winners.

Schaeffer & Long, Inc.
210 Davis Road
Magnolia, N.J. 08052
609-784-4044
MGRS: Fred Hoch & John Schaeffer. Specializes in complete restoration of antiques.

Vintage Auto Restorations
101 Atlantic Ave.
Spring Lake, N.J. 07762
201-449-8525
Complete and partial restorations.

NEW YORK

Del's Auto Body
112 Glen Street
Glen Cove, N.Y. 11542
516-OR 1-3130
OWNER/MGR: Del Mentnich. Specializes in the restoration of classics and vintage sports cars. No mechanical work.

Grand Prix SSR Co.
36 Route 25A
E. Setauket, N.Y. 11733
516-751-8700
Specializes in restoring Ferraris and other sports/racing cars.

Heritage Automotive Restorations
River Rd.
Pawling, N.Y.
914-855-5388

Speedwin Automotive Eng.
945 Motor Parkway
Hauppauge, N.Y. 11787
516-234-2400
Complete restorations.

OHIO

Paul Beechy
Winesburg, Ohio 44690

Budley & Sons
5599 Highland Road
Cleveland, O. 44143

Edward Cobb II Antique Auto Restoration
717 Western Ave.
Washington C.T., Ohio 43160
614-335-7489
Complete motor, transmission & differential rebuilding. Complete chassis restoration.

Feicht's Antique & Classic Auto Restoration
Columbiana, Ohio 44408
216-482-9221
Complete chassis restoration including engine, transmission and differential rebuilding.

Joseph R. McNutt
4228 State Road
Akron, O. 44119
Specializes in early Packards.

Vintage Auto Shop
430 Mill Street
Cincinnati, O. 45215
513-821-2159
            OWNER: Ned Herrmann. Specializes in Rolls-Royces.

OKLAHOMA
Classic Motors, Inc.
1046 N.W. 71st Street
Oklahoma City, Okla. 73116
405-848-2456

PENNSYLVANIA
Durland Edwards
350 Slocum Street
Swoyersville, Pa. 18704
            Antique and classic cars. 17 national first prize winners
for Tony Gould.

Fred Glazier, Jr.
Wambold Rd.
Souderton RD 1, Pa. 18964
215-723-8839
            Ford restorations; specializing in '32-'53 Ford V8s.

Richard's Auto Restoration
R.D. #3, Box 83A
Wyoming, Pa. 18644
717-333-4191
            OWNER: Richard Zimm. Restores antiques and classics.
Does no mechanical work or upholstery.

Stanley Sales and Service
C.S. Amsley, R.D. 2
Box 69
St. Thomas, Pa. 17252
            Complete steam car restoration.

Wilkinson & Sharp
233 Philmont Avenue
Feasterville, Pa. 19047
215-EL 7-8090
            MGRS: Stan Wilkinson & Arthur Sharp. Complete
antique and classic car restoration. Have restored cars for some of
the best known collectors in the U.S.

TEXAS
Classic Automobile Restoration Service
2810 Live Oak
Dallas, Tex. 75226
214-826-7188
            MGR: Bill Humphreys.

Coleman & Oquin Restoration
1569 Sheffield
Houston, Tex. 77015
713-455-2355
            Complete restoration of antique and vintage cars.

Jack Hildreth
7305 Lakehurst
Dallas, Tex. 75203
214-EM 9-2748

WISCONSIN

Dick's Autobody
Marshfield, Wis. 54449

Auto Strippers and Restorers, Inc.
900 W. Commerce St.
Cambria, Wis. 53923
414-348-5868
    Auto stripping and restoration.

CANADA

Fawcett Motor Carriage Works
Palmerston Avenue & Hgwy. 12
Whitby, Ontario
    OWNER: Ron Fawcett.

J. Brown Motors
Gorric, Ontario NOGIO
519-335-3325
    OWNERS: George and John Brown. Specializes in antique Fords.

Hugh McTavish
17 Wychwood Park
London, Ontario
    Specializes in antique engine rebuilding.

W.J. Oatman
75 Bartley Drive
Toronto 16, Ontario

Rose Saunders
Watford, Ontario

Appendix II:

Antique, Classic and Historic Car Clubs

GENERAL CLUBS

> **Antique Automobile Club of America**
> 501 W. Govenor Road
> Hershey, Pa. 17033

> **Classic Car Club of America***
> P.O. Box 443
> Madison, N.J. 07940

> **Contemporary Historical Vehicle Association**
> 71 Lucky Road
> Severn, Md. 21144

> **Horseless Carriage Club of America**
> 9031 E. Florence Avenue
> Downey, Cal. 90240

> **Milestone Car Society***
> Box 1166-L
> Pacific Palisades, Ca. 90272

> **The Society of Automotive Historians**
> Vernon W. Vogel, Secretary
> Box 24
> Edinboro, Pa. 16412

> **Steam Automobile Club of America, Inc.**
> 1937 E. 71st Street
> Chicago, Ill. 60649

> **Veteran Motor Car Club of America**
> 17 Pond Street
> Hingham, Mass. 02043

*Lists of eligible cars will be found at end of this section.

Vintage Sports Car Club of America
A.S. Carroll, Secretary
170 Wetherill Road
Garden City, N.Y. 11570

AC

AC Owners Club, American Centre
Danial G. Everett
Vinemont Road No. 6
Sinking Springs, Pa. 19608

ALFA ROMEO

Alfa Romeo Owners Club
Box 331
Northbrook, Ill. 60062

ALVIS

Alvis Owners Club
55 Motspur Park
New Malden, Surrey, England

AMERICAN AUSTIN/BANTAM

American Austin/Bantam
P.O. Box 328
Morris, N.Y. 13808

AMILCAR

Amilcar Register
27 Farnborough Crescent
Addington, Croydon, England

ARNOLT-BRISTOL

Arnolt-Bristol Registry
Robert Schifrin
9382 Gina Drive
West Chester, O. 45069

ASTON-MARTIN

Aston Martin Owners Club, Ltd.
Charles L. Turner
195 Mt. Paran Road, N.W.
Atlanta, Ga. 30327

AUBURN

Auburn-Cord-Duesenberg Club, Inc.
P.O. Box 11635
Palo Alto, Cal. 14306

BENTLEY

The Bentley Drivers Club
Andrew T. Fisher
317 Greenbank Ave.
Duarte, Cal. 91010

BUGATTI

The American Bugatti Club
8724 E. Garvey Avenue
Rosemead, Cal. 91770

Bugatti Owners Club
Sir Anthony Stamer, Secretary
Cedar Court, 9 The Fair Mile
Henley-on-Thames, Oxfordshire, RG9 2JT, England

BUICK

Buick Club of America
2765 Military Avenue
Los Angeles, Cal. 90064

Buick Collectors Club of America
Sidney Aberman
4730 Centre Avenue
Pittsburgh, Pa. 15213

CADILLAC

Cadillac Automobile Club
P.O. Box 2842
Pasadena, Cal. 91105

Cadillac La Salle Club
3340 Poplar Drive
Warren, Mich. 48091

CHEVROLET

The Vintage Chevrolet Club of America, Inc.
P.O. Box 1135
Bellflower, Cal. 90706

Vintage Chevrolet Club
1 Beechwood Avenue
Crescent Trailer Park
Gloucester, N.J. 08030

Vintage Corvette Club of America
c/o Ed Thiebaud
2359 W. Adams
Fresno, Cal. 93706

CHRYSLER

Chrysler 300 Club
c/o Ray Doern
4614 S.E. 32nd
Portland, Ore. 97202

Airflow Club of America
Chuck Cochran
Desoto Drive
O'Fallon, Ill. 62269

The W.P.C. Club (Walter P. Chrysler)
(Plymouth, Dodge, DeSoto, Chrysler, Imperial, and related cars)
17916 Trenton Drive
Castro Valley, Cal. 94546

Dodge, Chrysler, Plymouth, DeSoto, Maxwell Club
982 East 81st Street
Brooklyn, N.Y. 11236

Auburn-Cord-Duesenberg Club, Inc.
P.O. Box 11635
Palo Alto, Cal. 94306

CORD

See **"Duesenberg"**

CORVAIR

Corvair Society of America
209 Lyndhurst
Piqua, O. 45356

CROSLEY

Crosley Automobile Club
c/o John Aibel
15 Westminster Drive
Montville, N.J. 07045

DAIMLER

Daimler Club
c/o Gifford Dart
1500 Story Road
San Jose, Cal. 95122

DB

DB & Panhard Registry
See "**Panhard**"

DELAGE

Les Amis de Delage
Chateau des Ducs de Bretagne
44 Nantes, France

DODGE

Dodge, Chrysler, Plymouth, DeSoto, Maxwell Club
982 East 81st Street
Brooklyn, N.Y. 11236

DESOTO

DeSoto Club of America
P.O. Box 4912
Columbus, O. 43202

Dodge, Chrysler, Plymouth, DeSoto, Maxwell Club
982 East 81st Street
Brooklyn, N.Y. 11239

DUESENBERG

Auburn-Cord-Duesenberg Club, Inc.
P.O. Box 11635
Palo Alto, Cal. 94306

ESSEX

Hudson-Essex-Terraplane Club
7522 Canby No. 5
Reseda, Cal. 91335

FACEL

Facel Club
Richard A. Neary
528 Rahway Avenue
Woodbridge, N.J. 07095

FERRARI

Ferrari Club of America
Dyke Ridgley
1474 Greendell Dr.
Decatur, Ill. 62526

Ferrari Owners Club (G.B.)
Sir Anthony Stamer, Secretary
Cedar Court, 9 The Fair Mile
Henley-on-Thames, Oxfordshire RG9 2JT, England

Ferrari Owners Club (U.S.)
Ed Niles, Membership Chairman
3460 Wiltshire Blvd. Suite 1010
Los Angeles, Cal. 90010

FIAT

Fiat Club of America, Inc.
Box 192
Somerville, Mass. 02143

FORD

Model A Restorers Club, Inc.
Box 1930 A
Dearborn, Mich. 48121

Model A Ford Club of America
Box 2564
Pomona, Cal. 91766

Model T Ford Club International
c/o The Allerton
711 North Michigan Avenue
Chicago, Ill. 60611

The Model T Ford Club of America
P.O. Box 711
Tarzana, Cal. 91356

Early Ford Club (32-40)
P.O. Box 2122
San Leandro, Cal. 94577

Ford Mercury Club of America
P.O. Box 3551
Hayward, Cal. 94544

FRANKLIN

The H.H. Franklin Club
P.O. Box 66
Syracuse, N.Y. 13215

FRAZER

Kaiser-Frazer Owners Club
c/o Dick Enzel
8013 Glenhaven Road
Soquel, Cal. 95073

Kaiser-Frazer Owners Club of America, Inc.
Mr. Jesse E. Ehlers
4015 S. Forest
Independence, Miss. 64052

FRAZER-NASH

Frazer Nash Section of V.S.C.C.
20 School Hill
Walton le Wolds
Loughborough, Leics., England

G.M. CARS

General Motors Restorers Club
P.O. Box 307, Highland Station
Springfield, Mass. 01109

GRAHAM

Hupmobile-Graham Club of America

P.O. Box 215
Glenview, Ill. 60025

Graham & Graham-Paige Registry
Andrew Wittenborn
30 N. Broadway, Apt. 5E
White Plains, N.Y. 10601

HUDSON
Hudson-Essex-Terraplane Club
7522 Canby No. 5
Reseda, Cal. 91335

HUPMOBILE
Hupmobile-Graham Club of America
P.O. Box 215
Glenview, Ill. 60025

ISOTTA-FRASCHINI
Isotta-Fraschini Owners Association
9704 Illinois Street
Hebron, Ill. 60034

JAGUAR
EJAG North America
1 Acton Rd.
Westford, Mass. 01886

KAISER
Kaiser-Frazer Owners Club
c/o Dick Enzel
8013 Glenhaven Road
Soquel, Cal. 95073

Kaiser-Frazer Owners Club of America, Inc.
Mr. Jesse E. Ehlers
4015 S. Forest
Independence, Miss. 64052

KNIGHT
The Willys-Overland-Knight Registry
2754 Lullington Drive
Winston-Salem, N.C. 27103

LAGONDA
The Lagonda Club
R.T. Crane
10 Crestwood Trail
Lake Mohawk
Sparta, N.J. 07871

LANCIA
Lancia Motor Club
10 Arthur Road
Motspur Park, New Malden
Surrey, England

LA SALLE
Cadillac La Salle Club
3340 Poplar Drive
Warren, Mich. 48091

LINCOLN
Lincoln Continental Owners Club
P.O. Box 549
Nogales, Arizona 85621

Lincoln Zephyr Owners Club
6628 Verna Street
Library Street, Pa. 15129

MARMON
Marmon Owners Club
c/o Russell Stadt
5364 Stuart Avenue S.E.
Grand Rapids, Mich. 49508

MAXWELL
Dodge, Chrysler, Plymouth, DeSoto, *Maxwell* Club
982 East 81st Street
Brooklyn, N.Y. 11236

MERCEDES-BENZ
Mercedes-Benz Club of America
711 N. Institute
Colorado Springs
Colorado 80903

MERCURY
Ford Mercury Club of America
P.O. Box 3551
Hayward, Cal. 94544

MESSERSCHMITT
Messerschmitt Club
c/o Les Klinge
39 Sylvan Way
West Caldwell, N.J. 07006

M.G.
M.G. Car Club "Triple M" Register (Pre-War Only)
11 Orchard End Avenue
Amersham, Bucks., England

New England MG 'T' Register, Ltd.
Drawer #220
Oneonta, N.Y. 13820

NASH
Nash-Healey Car Club
Richard Kauffman, President
R.D. 2
Boyertown, Pa. 19512

Nash Car Club of America
635 Lloyd Street
Hubbard, O. 44425

OLDSMOBILE
Oldsmobile Club of America
P.O. Box 1498 Samp Mortar Station
Fairfield, Conn. 06430

OVERLAND
The Willys-Overland-Knight Registry
2754 Lullington Drive
Winston-Salem, N.C. 27103

PACKARD
Packard Automobile Classics

P.O. Box 2808
Oakland, Cal. 94618

Packards International Motor Car Club
P.O. Box 1347
Costa Mesa, Cal. 92626

PANHARD
DB & Panhard Registry
H.G. Schneider
Blair Academy
Blairstown, N.J. 07825

PIERCE-ARROW
Pierce-Arrow Society, Inc.
c/o Bernard J. Weis, Editor
135 Edgerton Street
Rochester, N.Y. 14607

PLYMOUTH
Dodge, Chrysler, Plymouth, DeSoto, Maxwell Club
982 East 81st Street
Brooklyn, N.Y. 11236

PORSCHE
Porsche Club of America
5616 Clermont Drive
Alexandria, Va. 22310

PLYMOUTH
Plymouth Owners Club
c/o R.E. Bender
Rd #1, Box 306
Jeannette, Pa. 15644

RAILTON
The Railton Owners Club
c/o Barrie McKenzie
Fairmiles
Barnes Hall Road
Burncross
Sheffield, S30 4RF, England

RILEY
The Riley R.M. Club
Mrs. D.M.E. Havart
1 The Crescent
Thurton, Norwich
Norfolk, Nor., 15W, England

ROLLS-ROYCE
Rolls-Royce Owners Club
1822 N. Second Street
Harrisburg, Pa. 17102

Rolls-Royce Enthusiasts Club
5 Halland Road
Leckhampton, Cheltenham, Glos., England

Rolls-Royce Section of Vintage Sports Car Club
The Malt House
Bewdley, Worcs., England

STEVENS-DURYEA
Stevens-Duryea Associates
Warwick Eastward
3565 Newhaven Road
Pasadena, Cal. 91107

STUDEBAKER
Studebaker Automobile Society
50 Hickory Drive
East Hartford, Conn. 06118

The Studebaker Driver's Club, Inc.
3328 Shorewood Drive
Mesquite, Tex. 75149

WILLYS
Willys Club of America
Ron Ladley
1117 Sydney St.
Philadelphia, Pa. 19150

The Willys-Overland-Knight Registry
2754 Lullington Drive
Winston-Salem, N.C. 27103

Classic Car Clubs of America:

Full Classic Marked: *
Part Classic Marked: in Detail
Non Classic Marked: No
A.C.*
Adler — Please apply.
Alfa Romeo*
Alvis — Speed 20, 25 and 4.3 litre.
Amilcar — Supercharged Sports
 Model*
 Others, please apply.
Apperson — No
Armstrong Siddeley — Please apply.
Aston-Martin — Ulster and Mark 2
 Team cars*
 Others, please apply.
Auburn — All Classic, except 6 cyl.
Austin (American) — No
Audi — No
Austro-Daimler*
Autovia — No
Bay State — No
Bentley*
Blackhawk*
B.M.W.* 327, 328 and 335 only.
Brewster — Heart Front Fords and one
 Heart Front Buick*
Bucciali*
Bugatti*
Buick — No, except one custom by
 Smith Bros.
Cadillac — All 1925 thru 1935*
 All 12's and 16's*
 1936-1942 — All 70, 72, 75, 80, 85,
 90*

All others are No, except five
 individual. 60's customs.
Case — No
Chandler — No
Chevrolet — No
Chrysler — 1926 thru 1930
 Imperial 80* 1931 Imp. 8 Series C.G.
 1932-C.G. and C.L. 1933-C.L.
 1934-C.W.-1935-C.W. & 5
 Newports and 6 Thunderbolts*
 All other — No
Citroen — No
Cleveland — No
Cole — No
Continental 1933 and 1934 — No
Continental Lincoln* Thru 1948.
Cord*
Cunningham*
Dagmar — 25-70 Model only*
Daimler — Please apply.
Darracq — 8 cyl. cars and 4 litre, 6
 cyl.*
 Others — No
Davis — No
Delage — 4 cyl. cars No
 Others, please apply.
Delahaye — 4 cyl. cars — No
 Others, please apply.
Delaunay Belleville — 6 cyl. cars*
 Others — No
De Soto — No
Devaux — No
Diana — No
Doble*

115

Dodge — No
Dorris*
Dort — No
Duesenberg*
du Pont*
Durant — No
Elcar — No
Erskine — No
Essex — No
Excelsior — Please apply.
Falcon Knight — No
Farman — Please apply.
Fiat — Please apply.
Flint — No
Ford — No
Franklin — all models* except 1933-34
   Olympic Sixes which are No
Frazer Nash — Please apply.
Gardner — No
Graham — No
Graham Paige — No, except 1929
   Graham Paige, LeBaron, D.C.
   Phaeton and 1930 G.P. Erdman and
   Rossi Conv. Vict.
Gray — No
Hansa Lloyd — No
Haynes — No
Hispano Suiza*
Horch*
Hotchkiss — Please apply.
Hudson — No, except 2 Biddle &
   Smart bodied "Greater Super
   Sixes."*
Hupmobile — No
Invicta*
Isotta Fraschini*
Itala*
Jensen — Please apply.
Jewett — No
Jordan — Speedway Series 'Z'* only.
   All others — No
Kissel — 1925 and 1926, 1927 — 8-75,
   1928, 8-90 and 8-90 White Eagle,
   1929 — 8-126 and 8-90 White Eagle,
   1930 — 8-126, 1931 — 8-126*
   All others — No
La Fayette — No
Lagonda*, except Rapier, which is No
Lammas-Graham — No
Lanchester — Please apply.
Lancia — Please apply.
La Salle — 1927 thru 1933* 1934 on —
   No.
Lexington — No
Lincoln — All K., L., K.A. and K.B.*
   1941 — 168H and 1942 — 268H*
   Zephyrs — No.
Locomobile — All models 48 and 90,
   1927 — 8-80, 1928 — 8-80, 1929 —
   8-80 and 8-88*
   All others — No

Marmon — All 16 cylinder* 1931 — 88
   and Big 8, 1930 — Big 8, 1928 —
   E75, 1927 — 75, 1925 and 1926 —
   74*
   Others — No
Marquette — No
Maxwell — No
Mayback*
McFarlan*
Mercedes Benz — All 230 and up, and
   S., S.S., S.S.K., S.S.K.L., Grosser
   and Mannheim*
Mercer*
M.G. — K3 Magnette*
   Others, please apply.
Minerva — 4 cyl. cars — No.
   Others*
Moon — if Custom, please apply.
   Others — No
Nash — No
Oakland — No
Oldsmobile — No
Opel — No
Overland — No
Packard — All sixes and eights 1925
   thru 1931 are*
   All twelves are*, 1932 — 900 (Light
   eight) is No. All 1932 — 901, 902,
   903, 904, 905 and 906 cars are*,
   as are all 1933 and 1934 cars,
   1935 etc. follows:

Classic
1935
1200, 1201, 1202, 1203, 1204, 1205, 1207
and 1208
1936
1400, 1401, 1402, 1403, 1404, 1405, 1407
and 1408.
1937
1500, 1501, 1502-1506, 1507 and 1508.
1938
1603, 1604, 1605, Super 1607 and 1608.
1939
1705 Super 1707 and 1708
1940
1806, 1807 and 1808 One-Eighty
1941
1906, 1907 and 1908 One-Eighty
1942
Super One-Eighty 2006, 2007 and 2008

Non-Classic
1935
120 8 cyl.
1936
120-B 8 cyl.
1937
115C 6 cyl., 120C 8 cyl., 120CD 8 cyl.,
   138CD 8 cyl.

1938
1600 6 cyl., 1601 8 cyl., 1601D 8 cyl., 1602 8 cyl.
1939
1700 6 cyl., One-Twenty, 1701 8 cyl., 1702 8 cyl., Super 1703 8 cyl.
1940
One-Ten, 1900 6 cyl., One-Twenty, 1901 8 cyl., One-Sixty, 1903 8 cyl., 1904 8 cyl., 1905 8 cyl., Clipper Eight, 8 cyl.
1942
Clipper Six, 2000 6 cyl., 2010 6 cyl., 2020 6 cyl., Clipper Eight, 2001 8 cyl., 2011 8 cyl., 2021 8 cyl., Super One-Sixty, 2003 8 cyl., 2023 8 cyl., 2004 8 cyl., 2005 8 cyl., 2055 8 cyl., 2030 8 cyl.

Paige — No
Peerless — Series 60, 1926-1928 and Custom 8, 1930 and 1931 and DeLuxe Custom 8, 1932*
  All others — No
Peugeot — Please apply.
Pierce-Arrow*
Plymouth — No
Pontiac — No
Railton — Please apply.
Renault — 45 HP*
  Others, please apply.
Reo — 1933 Royale Custom 8, 1930 and 1931 Royale Custom 8 and Series 8-35 and 8-52 Elite 8*
  All others — No
Revere*
Rickenbacker — No
Riley — Please apply.
Roamer — 1925 — 8-88, 6-54e and 4-75, 1926 — 4-75e and 8-88, 1927, 1928, 1929 — 8-88, 1929 — 8-125 and 1930 — 8-125*

All others — No
Rockne — No
Rohr*
Rollin — No
Rolls-Royce*
Roosevelt — No
Ruxton*
Salmson — No
Squire*
S.S. Jacuar — SS1, SS90 and SS100*
Star — No
Stearns Knight*
Sterling Knight — No
Stevens Duryea*
Steyr — Please apply.
Studebaker — No
Stutz*
Sunbeam — 8 cyl. and 3 twin cam*
  Others — No
Sunbeam Talbot — No
Talbot — 105 and 110 models*
  Others — No
Tatra — Please apply.
Terraplane — No
Triumph — Dolomite 8 and Gloria 6 models*
  Others — No
Vauxhall — 25-70 and 30-98*
  Others — No
Velie — No
Viking — No
Voisin*
Westcott — No
Whippet — No
Wills Saint Claire — All 1925 and 1926*
Willys — No
Willys Knight — No
Windsor — No

Milestone Car Society:

Eligible Cars:

Allard K2-K3   1952-55
Allard Series J   1946-55
Aston-Martin DB-1 — DB-4   1948-63
Bentley (ALL)   1946-64
Bugatti Type 101   1951
Buick Riviera   1949-63
Buick Skylark   1953
Cadillac Eldorado Brougham   1957-58
Cadillac (All except 75#) 1948-49
Chevrolet Corvette   1953-57
Chevrolet Nomad   1955-57
Chrysler Imperial   1951-54
Chrysler 300 — 300G   1955-61
Chrysler Town & Country   1946-50

Cisitalia GT Pininfarina   1946-49
Citroen D Series   1955-64
Continental Mark II   1956-57
Corvair Monza Spyder   1962-64
Cunningham (ALL)   1951-55
Delahaye Type 135-175-180   1946-51
Facel-Vega Excellence   1959-62
Facel-Vega FVS — HK500   1954-61
Facel II   1962-64
Ferrari 12   1947-64
Ford Skyliner Retractable   1957-59
Ford Thunderbird   1955-57
Frazer Manhattan   1947-50
Healey Silverstone   1949-50

Hudson Hornet   1951-54
Imperial (ALL)   1955-56
Jaguar XK-120   1948-54
Jaguar XK-E   1961-64
Kaiser Darrin 161   1953-54
Kaiser Deluxe/Virginian   1951-52
Kaiser Dragon   1951-53
Kaiser Manhattan   1954-55
Kaiser Vagabond   1949-50
Kaiser Virginian   1949-50
Lancia Flaminia Zagato   1959-64
Lincoln Capri   1952-54
Lincoln Continental   1947-48
Lincoln Continental   1961-64
Lotus Elite   1958-63
M.G. Midget Series TC   1946-49
Mercedes Benz 220S/SE coupe & conv.
   1957-64
Mercedes Benz 300 Sedan & Cabriolet
   1952-62
Mercedes Benz 300 S/Sc/SE/SL
   1952-64

Nash Healey (ALL)   1951-54
NSU Wankel Spyder   1964
Packard Caribbean   1953-56
Packard Custom   1946-50
Packard Pacific/Convertible   1954
Packard Patrician/Four Hundred
   1951-56
Pontiac Safari   1955-57
Porsche Series 356   1949-64
Riley 2.5   1945-55
Rolls-Royce (ALL)   1947-64
Studebaker Avanti   1963-64
Studebaker Gran Turismo Hawk
   1962-64
Studebaker Starliner Comm/Champ
   1953-54
Talbot-Lago 4.5 Grand Sport/Record
   1946-54
Tucker '48   1948
Willys Jeepster   1948-51
Woodill Wildfire   1952-58

Appendix III:

Restoration Services

ALUMINUM BODIES
Grand Prix SSR Co.
36 Rt. 25A
E. Setauket, N.Y. 11733
516-751-8700
Specialize in complete aluminum bodies, metal fabricating, heli-arc welding, etc.

AUCTIONS
Christie Manson & Woods U.S.A. Ltd.
867 Madison Avenue
New York, N.Y. 10021
212-744-4017

Kruse Classic Auction Co. Inc.
300 South Union Street
Auburn, Ind. 46706
219-925-4004

Sotheby Parke-Bernet, Inc.
980 Madison Avenue
New York, N.Y. 10021
212-TR 9-8300

BADGES-EMBLEMS-MASCOTS
I. Markovits Ltd.
1, 2, 3 Cobbold Mews
Longon, W.12
England

Pulfer & Williams
Robbins Rd.
Rd. 1
Rindge, N.H. 03461
603-899-5659

BEARINGS-POURED BABBIT
The Babbit Pot
Zigmont Bilus
52 Harrison Avenue
Glens Fall, N.Y. 12801
518-793-5411

119

Harking Machine Shop
115 1st Avenue NW
Watertown, S.D. 57201
605-886-7880

P & K Bearing
Sales and Service
5446 Penn Avenue
Pittsburgh, Pa. 15206
412-361-0116

BOOKS AND MANUALS

Classic Motorbooks
"Complete Stock of Books and Manuals"
P.O. Box 1
Osceola, Wisc. 54020
800-826-6600

R. Gordon & Co., Inc.
Auto Books and Magazines
12 East 55th Street
New York, N.Y. 10022
212-759-7443

The Kruse Green Book
"Market Prices of Antique and Classic Cars"
c/o Kruse Classic Auction Co.
300 South Union Street
Auburn, Ind. 46706

Rumbleseat Press
"All Ford Material"
6639 Blucher Avenue
Van Nuys, Cal. 91406

Crank'en Hope Publications
"Reprinted Manuals and Catalogs"
450 Maple Avenue
Box AJ-16
Blairsville, Pa. 15717
412-459-8853

Old Car Value Guide
P.O. Box 105
Prescott, Ariz. 86301
602-772-9625

Nat Adelstein
"Original Literature"
102 Farnsworth Avenue
Bordentown, N.J. 08505
609-888-1000

BRASS RESTORATION
Chris Music
957 Riverside
Fort Collins, Col. 80521

CAR COVERS
Warren Cox
P.O. Box 216
Lakewood, Cal. 90713
213-421-2884

Newco Car Covers
Cook Packing and Rubber
Box 286A
Leeds, Mass. 01053
413-586-0871

ELECTRICAL SYSTEMS
Harnesses Unlimited
Box 140
Plymouth Meeting, Pa. 19462

J.M.S. Antique Auto Parts Co.
3915 Kirkwood Highway
Wilmington, Dela. 19808
302-995-1131
   Custom harnesses & wiring supplies; custom braiding service.

Pacific Conduit and Cable
1725 Standard
Glendale, Calif. 91201
213-245-1013
   Auto wire and asphalt coated auto looms; harness braiding.

Wayne Schlotthauer
Wiring Diagrams
5815 Nielsen Drive
Paradise, Cal. 95969

The Wire King
P.O. Box 222
North Olmstead, O. 44070

ENGINE REBUILDING
Bill Drake's Engine Shop
15 Evelyn St.
Rochester, N.Y. 14606
716-458-0217

Grand Prix SSR Co.
36 Rte 25A
E. Setauket, N.Y. 11733
516-751-8700

H.R. Hendrix
"Ford A & B"
Rte. 1
Gray Court, S.C. 29645

Page's Model A
Haverhill, N.Y. 03765
no telephone
   Model A engine rebuilding.

Pioneer Valley Model A Ford
Warren Paul
178 Telegraph Ave.
Chicopee, Mass. 01020
413-533-2927
   Model A engine rebuilding.

The Restoration Engine Shop
R.D. 1, Box 228
Jamesburg, N.J. 08831
201-521-1128

Speedwin Automotive Engineering Restoration Division
945 Motor Parkway

Hauppauge, N.Y. 11787
516-234-2409

ENGINE TURNING (DAMASCENING)
Herb Newport
Box 100
Wittman, Md. 21676

FINANCING
Classic Car Finance Corp. Suite 440, 320 Interstate North
Atlanta, GA. 30339
404- 955-4431

Maryland National Bank

Collector Car Dept.
1713 West St.
Annapolis, MD. 21401
301-268-4343

GASKETS
Gerald J. Lettieri
132 Old Main Street
Rocky Hill, Conn. 06067
203-529-7177

Ace Gasket Co.
"Gaskets Made To Order"
244 W. Lincoln Avenue
Mt. Vernon, N.Y. 10550
914-MO 4-3710

Head Gasket Co.
c/o Fred Stelling
164 South Park
San Francisco, Cal. 94107

GAUGE REPAIRS
The Temperature Gauge Guy
45 Prospect Street
Essex Jct., Vt. 05452

J. Lynch
33 Loomis St.
Little Falls, N.Y. 13365
no telephone
Gauges, sending units, switches, hydro-electric window
cylinders repaired.

Nisonger Corp.
35 Bartels Pl.
New Rochelle, N.Y. 10801

Paul C. Sullivan
4311 Sunset Blvd.
Los Angeles, Cal. 90029

122

INSTRUMENTS RESTORED
John E. Marks
"Vintage Restorations of Instruments and Clocks"
4 Whybourne Crest
Tunbridge Wells
Kent TN2 5Bs, England
Tunbridge Wells 25899

Gus Scheuer
31 Dunwoodie Place
Greenwich, Ct. 06830
> Instrument dial face restoration.

INSURANCE
J.C. Taylor
8701 West Chester Pike
Upper Darby, Pa. 19082
215-853-1300

James A. Grundy Insurance
500 Office Center Drive
Fort Washington, Pa. 19034
215-628-3100

Condon and Skelly Insurance Brokers
P.O. Drawer "A"
Willingboro, N.J. 08046
609-871-1212

LEATHER
Connolly Bros. Ltd.
39-43 Chalton Street
London N.W.1, England

Harold Coker
Box 8056
Chattanooga, Tn. 37411
> Leather at wholesale prices.

Hides, Inc.
"Fine Upholstery Leather"
P.O. Box 30
Hackettstown, N.J. 07840

Bill Hirsch
396 Littleton Ave.
Newark, N.J. 07103
201-243-2858
> "Bridge of Weir" leather.

LEATHER PRESERVATIVE
Lexol Corp.
West Caldwell, N.J. 07006

LEATHER STRAPS & HARDWARE
Imcado Mfg. Co.
P.O. Box 452
Dover, Del. 19901

MACHINING
Walter Will
301 East 195th St.
Euclid, Oh. 44119
216-531-1631
> Machining of parts for antique and classic cars.

MAGAZINES •

Car and Parts
Box 299
Sesser, Ill. 62884

Hemming's Motor News
Box 380
Bennington, Vt. 05201

Special Interest Autos
Box 196
Bennington, Vt. 05201

Old Cars
Iola, Wis. 54945

MAGNETO/IGNITION COIL REPAIRS

George Pounden
1520 High School Road
Sebastopol, Cal. 94572
707-823-3824

METAL FABRICATION

Chester Auto Restoration Service
Perry Street
Chester, N.J. 07930
201-879-5041

MIRRORS-RESILVERED

Dan Tilstone
29 N. Delaware Rim Drive
Yardley, Pa. 19067
215-493-54

PARTS

Antique Auto Parts, Inc.
9113 E. Garvey Ave.
Rosemead, Cal. 91770
213-288-2121

Burchill Antique Auto Parts
4150 24 Ave. (U.S. 25 North)
Port Huron, Mich. 48060
313-385-3838

Classic Cars, Inc.
P.O. Box 56M
Morristown, N.J. 07960
201-538-1942

Egge Machine Co.
"Engine Parts"
8403 Allport
Sante Fe Springs, Cal. 90670
213-945-3419

J.C. Whitney & Co.
1917 Archer Avenue
Chicago, Ill. 60616

PARTS-AUBURN

Auburn / Cord Parts
604 South "G"
Wellington, Kan. 67152
316-326-7751

PARTS — BRASS
Monty Holmes
"Brass"
3653 Commodore Way
Seattle, Wash. 98199
206-282-4934

PARTS — CHEVROLET
Jim Tygart
Obsolete Chevrolet Parts Co.
P.O. Box 497
Nashville, Ga. 31639
912-686-5812

PARTS — CORD (SEE AUBURN)
Eric S. Cain
"The Cord Machine Shop"
9375 E. 12th
Tulsa, Okla. 74112
918-836-7385

PARTS — CORVETTES
T. Michaelis Corvette Supplies Inc.
Rt. 1, 424 East
Napoleon, Ohio 43545
800-537-3050
David N. Rosen
364 Tompkins Street
Cortland, N.Y. 13045

PARTS — ENGLISH CARS
The Complete Automobilist Ltd.
39 Main Street
Baston
Nr. Peterborough
PE6 9NX, England
Tel: Greatford 312

PARTS — FERRARI
David Clarke Ferrari Organization
Graypaul Motors Limited
Charnwood Road
Shepshed, Leics., England

FAF Motorcars Inc.
3862 Stephens Court
Tucker, Ga . 30084
404-939-5464

Grand Prix SSR Co.
36 Route 25A
E. Setauket, N.Y. 11733
516-751-8700

PARTS — FORD
A & L Parts Specialties
P.O. Box 301
Canton, Conn. 06019

Antique Auto & Parts by Pete
2144 West Superior Street
Chicago, Ill. 60612
312-486-1910

Antique Auto Parts
"Model 'T' Ford Parts"
173 Hotchkiss Street
Jamestown, N.Y. 14701

Antique Car Parts
Harold E. Severson
9400 S.E. 41st Street
Portland, Ore. 97222
503-659-2821

Antique Auto Specialties Co.
3803 15th Street "A"
Moline, Ill. 61265
309-794-0168

Beam Distributors
Davidson, N.C. 28036
704-892-8591

Bob's Antique Auto Parts
Box 1856
7826 Forest Hills Road
Rockford, Ill. 61110
815-633-7244

Dennis Carpenter
"V-8 Reproductions"
9835 Pinewood Lane
Charlotte, N.C. 28213

Classic Parts Center
"Thunderbird Parts"
916 San Mateo Ave.
San Bruno, Cal. 94066

The Craftsman's Guild
"Newood" Wood Parts
P.O. Box 63
Luna, N.M. 87824
505-547-2848

Pat Day Co.
"Genuine Ford Parts"
310 Rigsbee Avenue

Durham, N.C. 27702
919-688-2620

Bob Drake
"V-8 Reproductions"
P.O. Box 642
Woodland Hills, Cal. 91364

Ford Parts Obsolete, Inc.
1320 W. Willow
Long Beach, Cal. 90810

Gaslight Auto Parts, Inc.
P.O. Box 291
Urbana, O. 43078

Greenland Co.
P.O. Box 332
Verdugo City, Calif. 91046
213-249-8344

Mal's "A" Sales
4968 So. Pacheco Blvd.
Martinez, Cal. 94553

Mark Auto Co., Inc.
Layton, New Jersey 07851

Midwest Auto Parts Co.
P.O. Box 1081
Galesburg, Ill. 61401

Mike McKennett
"Restorations & Reproductions"
1250 N.W. Bella Vista Ave.
Gresham, Ore. 97030
503-666-3367

Model A Service
4727 S. 24th
Omaha, Neb. 68107

Page's Model A Garage
Main Street
Haverhill, N.H. 03765

Rick's Antique Auto Parts
Box 662
Shawnee Mission, Kan. 66201
800-255-4100

Snyder's Antique Auto Parts, Inc.
12925 Woodworth Road
New Springfield, O. 44443

Specialized Auto Parts, Inc.
301 Adams
Houston, Tex. 77011

Syverson Cabinet Co.
"Wood Parts That Fit to A T"
2301 Rand Road
Palatine, Ill. 60067

The V-8 Shop
8464 Riverview Road
Brecksville, O. 44141
216-526-7718

PARTS-JAGUAR

Bassett's Restorations and Supplies
P.O. Box 145
Peacedale, R.I. 02883
401-789-4110

PARTS — G.M. CARS

Warner Antique Car Parts Co.
4592 Warner Road
Cleveland, O. 44105
216-441-1960

PARTS — M.G. & ENGLISH CARS

Abingdon Spares Ltd.
1329 Highland Avenue
Needham, Mass. 02192
617-444-9235

Long's British Parts Ltd.
Box 19832
Kansas City, Mo. 64141

Moss Motors Ltd.
Box MG
Goleta, Cal. 93017
805-964-6969

Sports and Classics
750 Canal St.
Stamford, Conn. 06903
203-327-2775

Vintage Specialists
Box 225
Freeport, N.Y. 11520
516-868-6166

PISTONS

Jahn's Quality Pistons
2662 Lacy Street
Los Angeles, Cal. 90031
213-225-8177

Judson Mfg. Co., Inc.
1345 Byberry Road
Cornwells Heights, Pa. 19020

PLATING & POLISHING

Ace Chrome Plating Co.
728 W. Highland
Milwaukee, Wis. 53233
414-273-6596
        Chrome plating.

Bill's Metal Polishing
Davis Road & Camden Avenue
Magnolia, N.J. 08049
609-784-1019

Classic Custom Plating
North Wester at 71st
Oklahoma City, Okla. 73116
405-848-5717

Davison Plating Co.
845 N. State Rd.
Davison, Mich. 48423
313-653-4474
        Copper, nickel, chrome and brass plating on antique and classic cars.

Graves Plating Co.
Industrial Park
P.O. Box 1052H
Florence, Ala. 35630
205-764-9487
        Chrome plating antique cars.

High-Grade Plating Co.
1245 W. 2nd St.
Pomona, Calif. 91766
714-629-6616
        Chrome or nickel plating for antique cars; windshield frame and grille shell repair; headlight and reflector restoration.

Hygrade Polishing & Plating Co.
2207 41st Avenue
L.I. City, N.Y. 11101
212-EX 2-4082

J and J Chrome Plating
168 Peabody St.
West Haven, Ct. 06516
203-934-8510
    Chrome plating.

Modern Plating
242 So. 12th St.
Newark, N.J. 07107
201-638-8178
    Show chrome for antique cars.

O'Donnell Plating Shop, Inc.
41 A Mill St.
P.O. Box 33 Forest Park Station
Springfield, Mass. 01108
413-736-4303

R & S Chrome Plating
1933 Forster Street
Harrisburg, Pa. 17103
717-236-5693

Watervliet Plating Co.
911 11th Street
Watervliet, N.Y. 12189
518-273-1095

RADIO REPAIRS
Carl Heuther
(pre-1957 Car Radios)
Hobbs Road
Pelham, N.H. 03076
603-635-3048

Dan Packard
8 Florence Road
Marblehead, Mass. 01945
617-631-2449

Glen Thome
917 Delaware Ave.
Elyria, Oh. 44035
no telephone
    Radios repaired; any model, year.

RUBBER
The Complete Automobilist Ltd.
39 Main Street
Baston
Nr. Peterborough, PE6 9NX, England
Tel: Greatford 312

Metro Moulded Parts
P.O. Box 33098
Minneapolis, Minn. 55433

Lynn Steele
21144 Robinwood
Farmington, Mich. 48024

RUST REMOVAL
W.T. Tyrrel — PF-47 Rust Remover
Box 114
E. Northport, N.Y. 11731

"E Z" Truman
Sandblasters
1330 Market Street
Youngstown, O. 44507
216-743-9733
"Sand Blast Unit"
Lehman General Sales Co.
1835 Stelzer Road
Columbus, O. 43219

SHOCK ABSORBER RESTORATION
Classic Auto Shocks
17121 Palmdale
Huntington Beach, Cal. 92647
714-842-0707
J.D. Duke
1611 Brentwood
Athens, Tn. 37303
no telephone
> Model A shocks rebuilt.

STEERING WHEEL REPAIRS
Jim Ellis
P.O. Box 4633
Long Beach, Calif. 90804
213-586-3544
> Steering wheel restoration; repaired, refinished, recoated.

Steering Wheel Exchange
(Plastic Steering Wheels)
14214 E. Rosecrans Avenue
Lamirada, Cal. 90638
213-944-8549

TIMING CHAINS
Ramsey Products Corp.
724 Gesco Street
Charlotte, N.C. 28208
704-376-6477

TIRES
Bill's Antique Tires
P.O. Box 176
7526 Kay Lynn Street
Stanley, Kan. 66223
913-897-2685

Coker Tire Co., Inc.

5100 Brainerd Road
Chattanooga, Tenn. 37411
615-622-3191

Fred Kanter
Wide White Tire Co.
Box 33
Morris Plains, N.J. 07950
212-866-4605

John Kelsey
Kelsey Tire Co., Inc.
Box 564
Camdenton, Mo. 65020
314-346-2506

Lester Tire Co.
26881 Cannon Road
Bedford Hts., O. 44146
216-232-9030

Lucas Engineering
11848 W. Jefferson Blvd.
Culver City, Cal. 90230
213-397-3732

Universal Tire Co.
2650 Columbia Avenue
Lancaster, Pa. 17603
717-397-5184

Willie's Antique Tires
5257 W. Diversey Avenue
Chicago, Ill. 60639
312-622-4037

TITLES & REGISTRATIONS
Mac Charlson
113 Hinsdale
Mattydale, N.Y. 13211

TRAILERS
Bowsman Trailers
RR 4, Box 410
Three Rivers, Mich. 49093
616-279-5908

C & C Mfg. Co.
300 South Church Street
Hazeltown, Pa. 18201
717-454-0819

G. Sturgeon
3209 Erie Drive
Orchard Lake, Mich. 48033

Thomas O. Hudson
Tommy's Trailers
P.O. Box 71
Ada, Okla. 74802
405-332-7785

Trailex, Inc.
120 Industrial Park Drive
Canfield, O. 44406
216-533-6814

Wells Cargo, Inc.
"Enclosed Trailers"
1503 West McNaughton Street
Elkhart, Ind. 46514

UPHOLSTERY & TOP MATERIAL
Antique Fabric and Trim Co.
Rt. 2 — Box 870
Cambridge, Minn. 55008
612-742-4025

Bill Hirsch
396 Littleton Avenue
Newark, N.J. 07103
201-243-2858

131

Le Baron Bonney Co.
14 Washington Street
Amesbury, Mass. 01913

Charles (Wes) Salyer
P.O. Box 237
Kearney, Mo. 64060
816-676-2571

Stitts
Highway 23, Rt. 1
Churchtown, Pa. 17510
215-445-6821

UPHOLSTERY & TOP PATTERNS

Carters Cut and Cover Shop
Box 80
800 East 6th Street
Beardstown, Ill. 62618

WHEELS-WOOD

D.H. Arney
147 Carolynn Rd.
Mabank, Tex. 75147

Bob Calimer
30 East North St.
Waynesboro, Pa. 17268
717-762-5056

WIRE WHEELS

Dayton Wheel Products Inc.
2326 E. River Road
Dayton, O. 45439
513-294-7565

Wheel Repair Service Inc. of New England
176 Grove St.
Paxton, Mass. 01612
617-799-6551
Wire wheel rebuilding.

WOODGRAINING

James F. Cecil
906 Forest
Morristown, Tenn. 37814
615-586-3981

John R. Guerin
221 Herbert Avenue
Fanwood, N.J. 07023
201-889-6863

Realistic Woodgrain Concepts
P.O. Box 134
Centerville, Ohio 45459

Spectrum
P.O. Box 621
Auburn, Wash. 98002

WOOD TOP BOWS

Oak Bows
122 Ramsey Avenue
Chambersburg, Pa. 17201
717-264-2602

WOODWORK

C.B. Darcy
73 Scudders Lance
Glenhead, N.Y. 11545
no telephone   Custom automobile woodwork.